The Mission to
Mars and Beyond

General Editor

William H. Goetzmann
Jack S. Blanton, Sr., Chair in History
  University of Texas at Austin

Consulting Editor

Tom D. Crouch
Chairman, Department of Aeronautics
  National Air and Space Museum
  Smithsonian Institution

WORLD EXPLORERS

The Mission to
Mars and Beyond

Vincent V. DeSomma

Introductory Essay by Michael Collins

CHELSEA HOUSE PUBLISHERS

New York · Philadelphia

On the cover   Mars as seen from the *Viking* spacecraft

Chelsea House Publishers
Editor-in-Chief   Remmel Nunn
Managing Editor   Karyn Gullen Browne
Copy Chief   Mark Rifkin
Picture Editor   Adrian G. Allen
Art Director   Maria Epes
Assistant Art Director   Howard Brotman
Series Design   Loraine Machlin
Manufacturing Director   Gerald Levine
Systems Manager   Lindsey Ottman
Production Manager   Joseph Romano
Production Coordinator   Marie Claire Cebrián

World Explorers
Senior Editor   Sean Dolan

Staff for THE MISSION TO MARS AND BEYOND
Associate Editor   Terrance Dolan
Copy Editor   Christopher Duffy
Assistant Editor   Martin Mooney
Picture Researcher   Wendy Wills
Senior Designer   Basia Niemczyc

First Printing

1   3   5   7   9   8   6   4   2

Library of Congress Cataloging-in-Publication Data

DeSomma, Vincent V.
    The mission to Mars and beyond/Vincent V. DeSomma.
        p.   cm.—(World explorers)
    Includes bibliographical references and index.
    Summary: Discusses the proposed manned spaceflight to Mars and
what might be found there.
    ISBN 0-7910-1325-1
          0-7910-1549-1 (pbk.)
    1. Space flight to Mars—Juvenile literature.   2. Mars (Planet)—
Exploration—Juvenile literature.   [1. Space flight to Mars.
2. Mars (Planet)—Exploration.]   I. Title.   II. Series.
                                              91-31331
TL799.M3D47   1992   CIP
629.45'53—dc20   AC

CONTENTS

WORLD EXPLORERS

THE EARLY EXPLORERS

Herodotus and the Explorers of the Classical Age
Marco Polo and the Medieval Explorers
The Viking Explorers

THE FIRST GREAT AGE OF DISCOVERY

Jacques Cartier, Samuel de Champlain, and the Explorers of Canada
Christopher Columbus and the First Voyages to the New World
From Coronado to Escalante: The Explorers of the Spanish Southwest
Hernando de Soto and the Explorers of the American South
Sir Francis Drake and the Struggle for an Ocean Empire
Vasco da Gama and the Portuguese Explorers
La Salle and the Explorers of the Mississippi
Ferdinand Magellan and the Discovery of the World Ocean
Pizarro, Orellana, and the Exploration of the Amazon
The Search for the Northwest Passage
Giovanni da Verrazano and the Explorers of the Atlantic Coast

THE SECOND GREAT AGE OF DISCOVERY

Roald Amundsen and the Quest for the South Pole
Daniel Boone and the Opening of the Ohio Country
Captain James Cook and the Explorers of the Pacific
The Explorers of Alaska
John Charles Frémont and the Great Western Reconnaissance
Alexander von Humboldt, Colossus of Exploration
Lewis and Clark and the Route to the Pacific
Alexander Mackenzie and the Explorers of Canada
Robert Peary and the Quest for the North Pole
Zebulon Pike and the Explorers of the American Southwest
John Wesley Powell and the Great Surveys of the American West
Jedediah Smith and the Mountain Men of the American West
Henry Stanley and the European Explorers of Africa
Lt. Charles Wilkes and the Great U.S. Exploring Expedition

THE THIRD GREAT AGE OF DISCOVERY

Apollo to the Moon
The Explorers of the Undersea World
The First Men in Space
The Mission to Mars and Beyond
Probing Deep Space

CHELSEA HOUSE PUBLISHERS

Into the Unknown

Michael Collins

It is difficult to define most eras in history with any precision, but not so the space age. On October 4, 1957, it burst on us with little warning when the Soviet Union launched *Sputnik*, a 184-pound cannonball that circled the globe once every 96 minutes. Less than 4 years later, the Soviets followed this first primitive satellite with the flight of Yury Gagarin, a 27-year-old fighter pilot who became the first human to orbit the earth. The Soviet Union's success prompted President John F. Kennedy to decide that the United States should "land a man on the moon and return him safely to earth" before the end of the 1960s. We now had not only a space age but a space race.

I was born in 1930, exactly the right time to allow me to participate in Project Apollo, as the U.S. lunar program came to be known. As a young man growing up, I often found myself too young to do the things I wanted—or suddenly too old, as if someone had turned a switch at midnight. But for Apollo, 1930 was the perfect year to be born, and I was very lucky. In 1966 I enjoyed circling the earth for three days, and in 1969 I flew to the moon and laughed at the sight of the tiny earth, which I could cover with my thumbnail.

How the early explorers would have loved the view from space! With one glance Christopher Columbus could have plotted his course and reassured his crew that the world was indeed round. In 90 minutes Magellan could have looked down at every port of call in the *Victoria's* three-year circumnavigation of the globe. Given a chance to map their route from orbit, Lewis and Clark could have told President Jefferson that there was no easy Northwest Passage but that a continent of exquisite diversity awaited their scrutiny.

In a physical sense, we have already gone to most places that we can. That is not to say that there are not new adventures awaiting us deep in the sea or on the red plains of Mars, but more important than reaching new places will be understanding those we have already visited. There are vital gaps in our understanding of how our planet works as an ecosystem and how our planet fits into the infinite order of the universe. The next great age may well be the age of assimilation, in which we use microscope and telescope to evaluate what we have discovered and put that knowledge to use. The adventure of being first to reach may be replaced by the satisfaction of being first to grasp. Surely that is a form of exploration as vital to our well-being, and perhaps even survival, as the distinction of being the first to explore a specific geographical area.

The explorers whose stories are told in the books of this series did not just sail perilous seas, scale rugged mountains, traverse blistering deserts, dive to the depths of the ocean, or land on the moon. Their voyages and expeditions were journeys of mind as much as of time and distance, through which they—and all of mankind—were able to reach a greater understanding of our universe. That challenge remains, for all of us. The imperative is to see, to understand, to develop knowledge that others can use, to help nurture this planet that sustains us all. Perhaps being born in 1975 will be as lucky for a new generation of explorer as being born in 1930 was for Neil Armstrong, Buzz Aldrin, and Mike Collins.

The Reader's Journey

William H. Goetzmann

This volume is one of a series that takes us with the great explorers of the ages on bold journeys over the oceans and the continents and into outer space. As we travel along with these imaginative and courageous journeyers, we share their adventures and their knowledge. We also get a glimpse of that mysterious and inextinguishable fire that burned in the breast of men such as Magellan and Columbus—the fire that has propelled all those throughout the ages who have been driven to leave behind family and friends for a voyage into the unknown.

No one has ever satisfactorily explained the urge to explore, the drive to go to the "back of beyond." It is certain that it has been present in man almost since he began walking erect and first ventured across the African savannas. Sparks from that same fire fueled the transoceanic explorers of the Ice Age, who led their people across the vast plain that formed a land bridge between Asia and North America, and the astronauts and scientists who determined that man must reach the moon.

Besides an element of adventure, all exploration involves an element of mystery. We must not confuse exploration with discovery. Exploration is a purposeful human activity—a search for something. Discovery may be the end result of that search; it may also be an accident, as when Columbus found a whole new world while searching for the Indies. Often, the explorer may not even realize the full significance of what he has discovered, as was the case with Columbus. Exploration, on the other hand, is the product of a cultural or individual curiosity; it is a unique process that has enabled mankind to know and understand the world's oceans, continents, and polar regions. It is at the heart of scientific thinking. One of its most significant aspects is that it teaches people to ask the right questions; by doing so, it forces us to reevaluate what we think we know and understand. Thus knowledge progresses, and we are driven constantly to a new awareness and appreciation of the universe in all its infinite variety.

The motivation for exploration is not always pure. In his fascination with the new, man often forgets that others have been there before him. For example, the popular notion of the discovery of America overlooks the complex Indian civilizations that had existed there for thousands of years before the arrival of Europeans. Man's desire for conquest, riches, and fame is often linked inextricably with his quest for the unknown, but a story that touches so closely on the human essence must of necessity treat war as well as peace, avarice with generosity, both pride and humility, frailty and greatness. The story of exploration is above all a story of humanity and of man's understanding of his place in the universe.

The WORLD EXPLORERS series has been divided into four sections. The first treats the explorers of the ancient world, the Viking explorers of the 9th through the 11th centuries, and Marco Polo and the medieval explorers. The rest of the series is divided into three great ages of exploration. The first is the era of Columbus and Magellan: the period spanning the 15th and 16th centuries, which saw the discovery and exploration of the New World and the world ocean. The second might be called the age of science and imperialism, the era made possible by the scientific advances of the 17th century, which witnessed the discovery of the world's last two undiscovered continents, Australia and Antarctica, the mapping of all the continents and oceans, and the establishment of colonies all over the world. The third great age refers to the most ambitious quests of the 20th century—the probing of space and of the ocean's depths.

As we reach out into the darkness of outer space and other galaxies, we come to better understand how our ancestors confronted *oecumene,* or the vast earthly unknown. We learn once again the meaning of an unknown 18th-century sea captain's advice to navigators:

> And if by chance you make a landfall on the shores of another sea in a far country inhabited by savages and barbarians, remember you this: the greatest danger and the surest hope lies not with fires and arrows but in the quicksilver hearts of men.

At its core, exploration is a series of moral dramas. But it is these dramas, involving new lands, new people, and exotic ecosystems of staggering beauty, that make the explorers' stories not only moral tales but also some of the greatest adventure stories ever recorded. They represent the process of learning in its most expansive and vivid forms. We see that real life, past and present, transcends even the adventures of the starship *Enterprise.*

Planet of the Imagination

Each of the nine planets in our solar system exerts a gravitational influence on its neighboring planets and moons. Jupiter, the largest of the nine, has the strongest gravity. Tiny Pluto, the outermost planet, has the weakest. Each planet also exerts a certain influence on the human imagination. Mercury, closest to the sun, is perceived as a hellish place of heat and fire. Brilliant Venus is an alluring beacon, outshining any object in our sky except for the sun and the moon. After Earth and its sister planet, Mars, come the massive outer, or Jovian planets: godlike Jupiter, swathed in a colorful, swirling, frosty atmosphere and accompanied by a retinue of 16 moons; gigantic, beautiful Saturn with its spectacular system of rings; icy, pale green Uranus; cool, distant Neptune, first seen by Galileo in 1612; and finally minuscule Pluto, guardian of the dark, maintaining a lonely orbital vigil far from the warming heat of the sun.

But it is Mars, the fourth planet from the sun, that exerts the greatest influence on the collective imagination of humankind. Throughout history our thoughts have gravitated to Mars, pulled toward the red planet as if by some unseen force. Named for the Roman god of war because of its lurid reddish hue, no other planet has occupied such a significant place in earthly culture. Astronomers and planetary scientists of the late 20th century have

Mars, Earth's sister planet, has always attracted the attention and stimulated the imagination of humankind. Musing about the possible inhabitants of the red planet in The Martian Chronicles, *fantasist Ray Bradbury wrote, "They had a house of crystal pillars on the planet Mars by the edge of an empty sea."*

acquired a considerable amount of concrete information about Mars, but earlier observers and theorists, lacking today's sophisticated instruments, filled in the gaps in their knowledge of the planet with speculation, which was embellished down the years by charlatans, fantasists, science fiction writers, and, eventually, television producers and filmmakers. Mars acquired a multitude of "histories" centuries before the first unmanned spacecraft from Earth (*Viking 1*) made a successful landing on its rusty, arid plains in 1975. Indeed, residents of a certain New Jersey town still talk about the terrible war fought between earthlings and Martians back in 1938.

Martians—that is the word that sets Mars apart from the other planets in our solar system, the word that has given the planet its special gravity. Nobody knows who coined the word, but it became common in the 19th century when improved telescopes and the red planet's proximity to Earth allowed astronomers to study the surface of Mars more closely than ever before. Earlier astronomers such as Galileo Galilei, Christian Huygens, and William Herschel had already observed certain striking similarities between Earth and Mars. Both planets rotate on an axis and have 24-hour days. Both planets are tilted on their axis at an angle of 23 degrees. Mars, like Earth, has an atmosphere, polar ice caps, and four seasons. If Mars had such things in common with Earth, it was not unreasonable to think that it might have inhabitants—Martians—as well. And in the latter part of the 19th century two men made startling observations that seemed to suggest strongly that Mars did indeed host intelligent life.

In 1877, Giovanni Virginio Schiaparelli, the highly respected director of Italy's Milan observatory, trained a telescope on Mars. The red planet's elliptical orbit was bringing it relatively close to Earth that year, and Schiaparelli intended to take advantage of the opportunity. One particularly clear night, as he studied the planet's surface through an eight-inch telescope, the Italian saw a network

Because of its bloody hue, planet Mars was named after the Roman god of war, seen here as portrayed by the great 17th-century Flemish painter Peter Paul Rubens. The ancient Sumerian, Babylonian, Persian, Egyptian, and Greek cultures all associated the red planet with battle, death, blood, and fire.

of dark grooves or lines covering the face of Mars. The lines connected large dark areas on the planet's surface, which were thought by many observers to be Martian seas or oceans. When he reported his observation to other scientists and astronomers, Schiaparelli referred to the lines as *canali*, a word that, in Italian, does not necessarily mean "canals"; it can also mean "channels" or "grooves." But the astronomer's colleagues, and the public, seemed to choose the "canals" interpretation.

Canal connotes an artificial waterway, something that is built rather than something that occurs naturally, and so it was logically assumed that any canals on Mars had been built by Martians. Thus was born the theory—or legend—of the canals of Mars and the great Martian engineers. Over the years, the myth of the Martian canals grew to be so pervasive that the two words, *Mars* and *canal*, became inextricably linked. In *Webster's Ninth New Collegiate Dictionary*, published in 1985, the fourth definition for *canal* is "any of various faint narrow markings held to exist on the planet Mars."

The careful Giovanni Schiaparelli would neither endorse nor dismiss the theory of an artificial origin for the Martian canals, but the idea itself was to prove strangely popular and quite resilient. A French astronomer told Schiaparelli that "your observations have made Mars the most interesting point for us in the entire heavens." As word of the canals spread, self-styled astronomers and planetologists everywhere were putting their telescopes and imaginations to work. The idea of life on another planet had struck a chord—it almost seemed that the human race was terribly lonely, desperate for cosmic kin, or at least cosmic neighbors. One of these hopeful Mars watchers was an American.

Maps drawn by Italian astronomer Giovanni Schiaparelli in 1890 show the infamous Martian "canals"—long, interconnected grooves on the face of the planet, observed by the astronomer through a telescope. "There are on this planet," wrote Schiaparelli, "long dark lines which may be designated as canali."

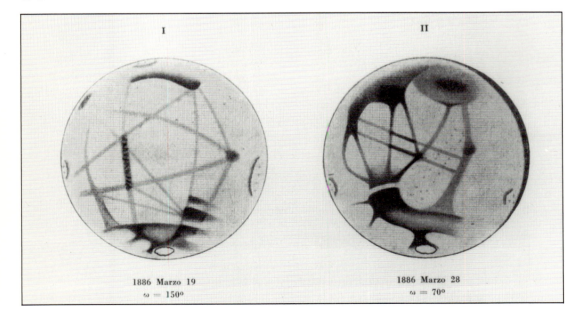

I   II

1886 Marzo 19   1886 Marzo 28
ω = 150°   ω = 70°

Percival Lowell was a man with a lot of time on his hands. A wealthy Bostonian of a somewhat whimsical nature, Lowell graduated from Harvard in 1876 and spent the next 10 years traveling at his leisure about Europe and Asia and then writing books about his journeys. At some point during his travels, Lowell became obsessed with the planet Mars; most likely he read a newspaper report about Schiaparelli's canals. Returning to the United States, Lowell built an observatory on a knoll near Flagstaff, Arizona. He named the place Mars Hill. Night after night, month after month, year after year Lowell scrutinized the red planet from his desert observatory.

In 1895, Lowell published his findings in a book, *Mars*. Schiaparelli had indeed observed artificial canals on Mars, Lowell asserted. The planet, according to Lowell, was clearly marked with an extensive, global network of at least 184 canals. Not only were the canals real, *Mars* concluded, they were the work of an intelligent race of master engineers—Martians. Lowell even had a theory about the purpose of these Martian waterways. Mars, he claimed,

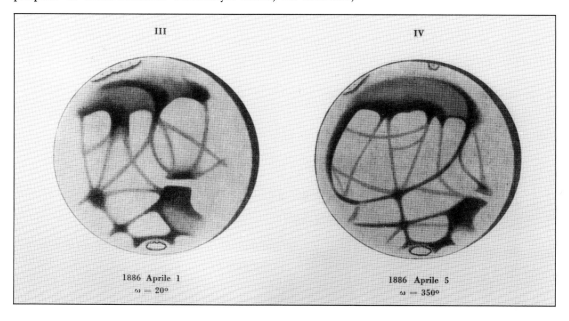

III

IV

1886 Aprile 1
ω = 20°

1886 Aprile 5
ω = 350°

was parched and arid, a planet dying of thirst. Its only remaining water resources were the polar ice caps, which were clearly visible from earth. The Martians, in a desperate, heroic effort to save their civilization, had constructed a planet-wide irrigation network—the canals—to channel water from the poles to the harsh, barren deserts.

Lowell's theories were eagerly embraced by the general public. The scientific community was not so supportive, and as the years went by his canals were increasingly dismissed as optical illusions or the product of wishful thinking. But Lowell clung to his Martian visions, and when he died in 1916—he was interred on Mars Hill—they did not die with him, for they had already assumed a life of their own in the popular imagination. It seems that while Lowell was watching Mars, the Martians were watching Earth. According to science fiction writer H. G. Wells, "in the early years of the Twentieth century this world was being watched closely by intelligences greater than man's and yet as mortal as his own. . . . [I]ntellects vast, cool, and unsympathetic regarded this earth with envious eyes and slowly and surely drew their plans against us." Twenty-two years after the death of Percival Lowell, the Martians arrived on earth. They landed first near a small town in New Jersey called Grovers Mill, and they were not in a friendly mood.

"Ladies and gentlemen, I have a grave announcement to make. Incredible as it may seem, both the observations of science and the evidence of our eyes lead to the inescapable assumption that those strange beings who landed in the Jersey farmlands tonight are the vanguard of an invading army from the planet Mars. The battle which took place tonight in Grovers Mill has ended in one of the most startling defeats ever suffered by an army in modern times; seven thousand men armed with rifles and machine guns pitted against a single fighting machine of the invaders from Mars. One hundred and twenty known sur-

vivors. The rest strewn over the battle area from Grovers Mill to Plainsboro crushed and trampled to death under the metal feet of the monster, or burned to cinders by its heat-ray. The monster is now in control of the middle section of New Jersey. Communication lines are down from Pennsylvania to the Atlantic Ocean."

Astronomer Percival Lowell studies his idée fixe through a telescope at Mars Hill observatory. "The broad physical conditions of the planet," he argued, "are not antagonistic to some form of life."

This was part of the chilling "news report" thousands of Americans heard over the radio on the night of October 30, 1938. As word of the "invasion" spread, an hour or two of acute panic struck the East Coast of the United States. Frightened citizens—in New Jersey especially—took to the streets and fled, abandoning their homes to the oncoming "monsters." Those who stayed by their radios to listen to news coverage of the event heard a series of bulletins that described the Martians' destructive march on New York City, where crowds of people supposedly

"For want of a better term, I shall refer to the mysterious weapon as a heat-ray. It's all too evident that these creatures have scientific knowledge far in advance of our own . . ." spoke a character in the Mercury Theatre radio play based on H. G. Wells's science fiction novel The War of the Worlds. Seen here is an illustration from Wells's novel.

were jumping into the East River to escape the fearful "heat-rays." It was the end of the world; Lowell's Martians had come. Maybe their canals had finally run dry.

The great Halloween hoax of 1938 was the product of the popular "Mercury Theatre on the Air" live-drama radio show and of the mischievous imagination of Orson Welles, a clever young writer and director for the Mercury Theatre. But Welles never dreamed that his hour-long adaptation of *The War of the Worlds*, a science fiction novel by H. G. Wells, would elicit such a response. Sociologists have attributed the panic to Welles's creative and effective use of the radio medium and also to the invasion paranoia and prewar jitters Americans were suffering from as the outrages of Nazi dictator Adolf Hitler of Germany threatened to spark a global confict. But the incident also showed that the concept of *Mars* and *Martians* had assumed a rather powerful place in the popular culture of early 20th-century America. A radio report about an invasion from Venus or Jupiter would not have been taken so seriously.

At the end of *The War of the Worlds* the invading Martians are killed off by bacteria that humans are immune to, and Earth is saved. And so one of the first of many "histories" of Mars and the Martians was resolved. But, as the fictional radio announcer asserted, these Martians were but the "vanguard of an invading army from the planet Mars." As the 20th century wore on, the Martians continued to come. In comic books and in magazines, in short stories and in novels, on radio and television and in the movies, the Martians arrived. Tales of planet Mars abounded as well. It was a place of red deserts; of towering cities; of lost civilizations; it was a paradise and it was a hell. Mars had become, by the 1950s, the repository of earthly hopes, fears, and dreams. But there were humans who were not satisfied with hopes and dreams. And, by the end of the fifties, there were rockets.

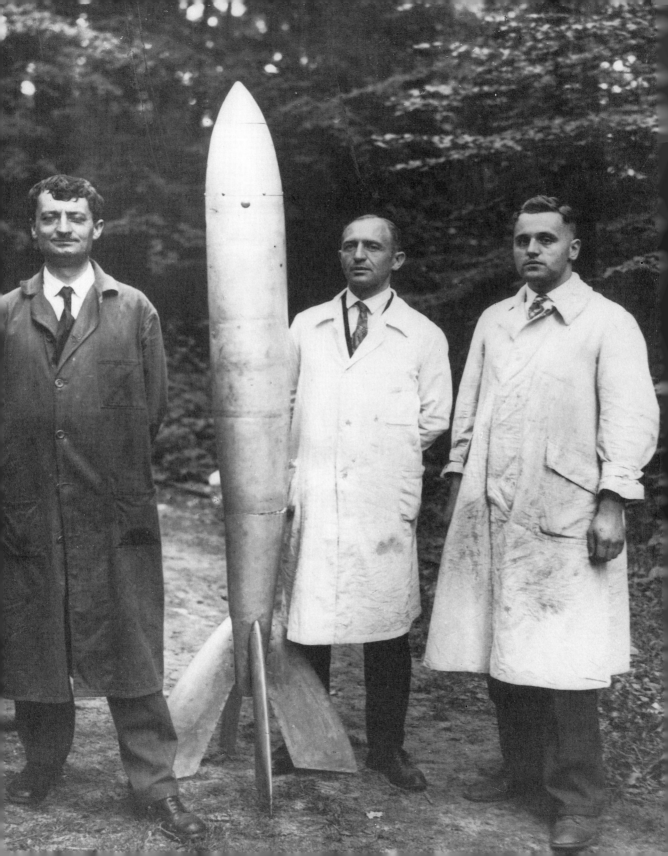

Rockets, Men, and Robots

In 1903, a Russian named Konstantin Tsiolkovsky wrote a science fiction novel about rockets and spaceflight that was based on his own research into the principles of jet propulsion. In 1911, just three years after Percival Lowell published his book *Mars as the Abode of Life*, Tsiolkovsky published the first practical manual on spaceflight, *Exploration of Cosmic Space with Reactive Devices*. In 1926, residents of a Massachusetts town called Auburn were astonished when a small streamlined object hissed into the sky from somewhere nearby. The object—the world's first liquid-propelled rocket—had been designed, built, and launched by Robert H. Goddard from his aunt Effie's backyard. Goddard, who had studied the theories of Tsiolkovsky, continued his pioneering research until his death in 1945. By then he was known as the father of American rocketry.

In the meantime, a Romanian scientist, Dr. Hermann Oberth, wrote a small book called *The Rocket into Interplanetary Space*, which was based on the ideas of Tsiolkovsky and the research of Goddard. Oberth's book was instrumental in bringing the principles and theories of rocketry to the attention of innovative scientists and engineers around the world. Among these original rocketeers was a German named Wernher von Braun. Von Braun, a gifted engineer and physicist, read Oberth's book and

Pioneer rocket scientist Hermann Oberth (left) and two assistants pose for a photograph with a small rocket in 1931. "How they goin' to get to Mars?" one disbelieving character asks in Ray Bradbury's Martian Chronicles. *"Rockets," answers another.*

was intrigued. He joined the Society for Space Travel, founded by Oberth and located in Berlin. Building and launching rockets with Oberth at the Berlin *Raketenflug-platz* (rocket testing field), von Braun and the other members of the society drew the attention of the German authorities, who in 1933 put them to work designing missiles for the German military.

When World War II ended, von Braun fled to the United States, where, under the auspices of the U.S. military, he continued his work on rockets. Many of the original members of the Society for Space Travel came to the United States with von Braun after the war; others went to the Soviet Union, where they joined the burgeoning Soviet rocket program, which was run by Sergey Korolyov, the famed "chief designer." The result of this

Dr. Robert Goddard (second from right) and fellow rocketeers prepare to place a test rocket in a launch tower at Roswell, New Mexico, in 1931. Goddard's interest in rockets began at the age of 16 when he sat in a cherry tree and read a science fiction story about interplanetary travel. "I was a different boy when I descended that tree," he recalled years later.

infusion of German technical know-how into the Soviet and American postwar rocket programs was the dawning of the space age.

October 4, 1957, is usually cited as the date on which the space age began. On that day, the Soviet Union, using a liquid-propelled rocket, launched and put into Earth orbit the first artificial satellite, *Sputnik 1*. Realizing that the United States was falling behind its cold war antagonist in the field of rocket development and space exploration, President Dwight D. Eisenhower formed the National Aeronautics and Space Administration (NASA) and assigned it the task of putting a man into space before the Soviets. The space race had begun. Less than four years later, on April 12, 1961, cosmonaut Yury Gagarin of the Soviet Union became the first human being in outer space (and the first true space-age hero), orbiting the Earth once in *Vostok 1*, a crude, spherical spacecraft that had been boosted out of the atmosphere by an A-1 rocket. NASA scrambled to get an American into space (Alan Shepard was the first, May 4, 1961), and President John F. Kennedy, hoping to upstage the Soviets, declared that the United States would put a man on the moon by the end of the decade. Soviet premier Nikita Khrushchev also had lunar ambitions, and the Soviets began their own moon effort.

The term *space race* generally brings to mind the contest between the United States and the Soviet Union to put a man in Earth orbit and then to send a man to the moon. But there was another aspect to the space race, although this part of the competition was (and still is) overshadowed by the more glamorous manned programs of the two superpowers. Despite the focus on the moon, it was inevitable that once rockets that could carry a payload into outer space were developed, humans would begin attempts to reach Mars. At the beginning of the space race, sending a human being to Mars was not feasible technologically—the red planet was simply too far away. A manned flight

Soviet cosmonaut Yury Gagarin became the world's first space-age hero when he orbited Earth in the spacecraft Vostok 1 *on April 12, 1961. "To be the first man in space—to meet nature face to face in an unprecedented encounter—could one dream of anything greater?" Gagarin asked shortly before his historic flight.*

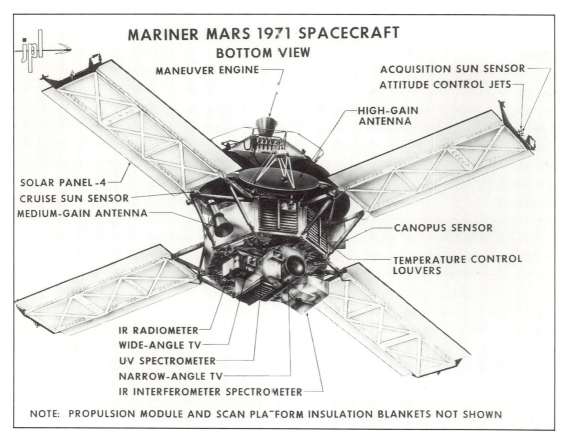

MARINER MARS 1971 SPACECRAFT
BOTTOM VIEW

MANEUVER ENGINE

ACQUISITION SUN SENSOR
ATTITUDE CONTROL JETS

HIGH-GAIN ANTENNA

SOLAR PANEL -4
CRUISE SUN SENSOR
MEDIUM-GAIN ANTENNA

CANOPUS SENSOR

TEMPERATURE CONTROL LOUVERS

IR RADIOMETER
WIDE-ANGLE TV
UV SPECTROMETER
NARROW-ANGLE TV
IR INTERFEROMETER SPECTROMETER

NOTE: PROPULSION MODULE AND SCAN PLATFORM INSULATION BLANKETS NOT SHOWN

Four of NASA's "flying windmill" Mariner probes engaged in aerial reconnaissance of Mars. In 1971, Mariner 9 became the first spacecraft to orbit the planet. Its two television cameras, peering down at the planet's surface through Martian dust storms, revealed an awe-inspiring terrain.

to the moon, which is roughly 230,000 miles away from Earth, takes at least 3 days. A manned one-way flight to Mars, which is 35 million miles away at its closest approach to our planet, could take up to a year. Consequently, both the U.S. and Soviet space agencies focused on the moon as a goal for their manned spaceflight programs. But Mars was not forgotten, and if humans could not yet go there, the next best thing—robotic probes—might be sent to the red planet instead. So, while the Soviet and American space agencies were engaged in a manned race to Earth orbit and then to the moon, they were also involved in a contest to send unmanned probes to Mars.

The Soviets, who had gotten a head start in the manned space race, hoped to jump out in front of the United States in the unmanned race to Mars as well. From 1960 to 1964, the Soviet Union mounted an intensive effort to reach Mars with an unmanned spacecraft. Six missions were launched; all six failed. The first four missions suffered from booster-rocket problems. Only two of the Mars probes—*Mars 1*, launched in November 1962, and *Zond 2*, launched in 1964—made it out of Earth's atmosphere, and they both malfunctioned during the long voyage to Mars. It was a dismal time for the Soviet scientists, engineers, technicians, and flight directors who were involved in the Mars program. They returned to their blackboards, leaving the field open to their rivals.

NASA was ready. The *Mariner* planetary probe, the result of a joint research and development project undertaken by NASA, the California Institute of Technology, and the Jet Propulsion Laboratory in Pasadena, California, was deemed spaceworthy in the fall of 1964, and a November 5 launch date was set. The *Mariner* spacecraft—as well as all of the other unmanned spacecraft sent to explore the solar system—was, in effect, a mechanical extension of human perception. These little interplanetary travelers were the surrogate eyes of humanity, sent to take a look at mysterious Mars.

Weighing 575 pounds and measuring a little more than 22 feet across, the *Mariner* has been described as having the appearance of a flying windmill. Its design was purely functional and consisted of a metallic, octagonal body; four solar panels (the vanes of the "windmill") for power; a high-gain antenna for receiving radio commands from Earth and a transmitter for sending data back to Earth; and small cold-gas rockets for course adjustments. *Mariner* also carried a computer, a star tracker, and six devices that would measure cosmic rays, solar wind, magnetic fields, and micrometeorite density. But the most important element of the spacecraft was the television camera—the "eyes" that would allow humans to get the first close-up look at Mars.

The first scheduled Mars probe, *Mariner 3*, suffered a launch failure on November 5, 1964, but three weeks later an *Atlas/Agena* rocket boosted its twin, *Mariner 4*, out of Earth's atmosphere and sent it on its way to Mars. Three hundred and twenty-five million miles and 228 days later, *Mariner 4* made the first flyby of the red planet. Hurtling past the planet at a distance of 6,118 miles, *Mariner 4* took 22 photographs and began transmitting the images, in a digital computer code, back to Earth, where they were reconstituted on photographic film. This was a long, painstaking process, and scientists at the Jet Propulsion Laboratory watched impatiently over the next two weeks as the images of Mars gradually took shape. (*Mariner 4*, its task completed, was left in a slowly decaying Mars orbit, which was a rather melancholy concept for many of the people who had worked on the project from the beginning.)

The images of Mars transmitted back to Earth from *Mariner 4* showed a bleak, sun-blasted, cratered surface. There were no canals; in fact, the planet seemed entirely waterless, which was a great disappointment to those who had hoped to see a Mars that might support some kind of life. Most exobiologists (scientists involved in the search for extraterrestrial life) agreed that without water there was little chance of life-forms of any kind existing on Mars. *Mariner 4* had only photographed a tiny area of the Martian surface, however, and plans for three more *Mariner* missions were soon being made. While NASA's Apollo and Gemini programs were bringing astronauts closer and closer to the moon, the Mars cabal at the Jet Propulsion Laboratory quietly prepared *Mariner 6* and *Mariner 7*. On July 30, 1969, just 10 days after Neil Armstrong walked the surface of the moon, *Mariner 6* completed a successful Mars flyby, and a week later *Mariner 7* followed. The two

Mariners passed within 2,500 miles of the Martian surface and took more than 200 photographs of the planet's southern hemisphere. Little by little, Earth's scientists were getting to know Mars.

Mariner 9, a Mars orbiter, was launched in May 1971. On November 13, 1971, it became the first man-made object to orbit a planet other than Earth. Mariner 9 circled Mars for almost a year before it finally ran out of fuel for

The control room at Pasadena's Jet Propulsion Laboratory served as the "brain" for the Mariner probes. Flight controllers directed and monitored the probes on a 24-hour basis for the duration of the missions, receiving daily images of the red planet.

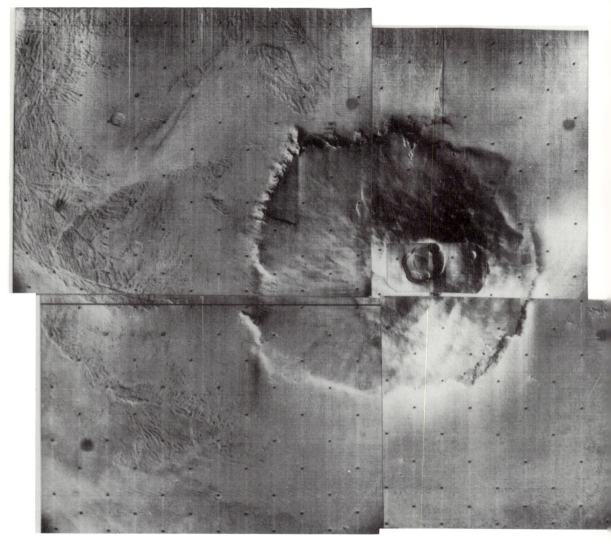

Some of the more startling images to be transmitted back to Earth from Mariner 9 *showed* Olympus Mons, *a volcano of staggering proportions located in the northern hemisphere of Mars.*

its attitude-control thrusters (small jets that allowed flight controllers to keep the spacecraft in the correct position) and went into an irreversible tumble. During its orbital reconnaissance, *Mariner 9* took more than 7,000 photographs of the planet's surface. It was an unprecedented wealth of information, and it allowed planetary scientists to complete a global map of Mars. Exultant planetary geologists regarded the continuing stream of information coming back to Earth from *Mariner 9* as a revelation.

As the probe continued to photograph and transmit, it became increasingly apparent that the surface of Mars had a much more varied and unexpected makeup than any-one—including even Percival Lowell—had previously imagined. Instead of the desolate, cratered, radiation-blasted global desert implied by the early *Mariners*, the photographs now began to show remarkable features. Mars was still a harsh, dry, dead planet, but now scientists were seeing a topography that suggested that Mars might once have been an entirely different world—a living, watery planet like Earth. Pictures of the previously unphoto-graphed northern hemisphere of Mars showed evidence of massive flooding—canyons, flood channels, deltas, drainage systems, and broad flood plains. There was also clear evidence of volcanism on Mars, including one vol-cano that was larger than even the most imaginative of fantasists might have conjured in a comic book or novel.

While the *Mariners* were supplying American scientists with a windfall of Mars data, the Soviets were attempting to revive their own Mars program. But troublesome tech-nology—or perhaps simply bad luck—continued to ham-per their efforts. In May 1971, at the same time that *Mariner 9* orbited Mars, two Soviet spacecraft converged on the red planet. These new Soviet craft were landers, not simply orbiters like the *Mariners*. The Soviets had designed three probes—*Kosmos*, *Mars 2*, and *Mars 3*—to actually land on Mars, an accomplishment that would catapult the Soviet Mars program past NASA's effort. But *Kosmos* suffered launch failure, and *Mars 2* and *Mars 3* did not survive their landing on the Martian surface. Two additional *Mars* landers failed in 1973; the Soviets, re-buffed by Mars yet again, would make no more attempts to explore the red planet until 1988.

Life on Mars?

At NASA, the revelations of *Mariner 9* stimulated new interest in Mars, particularly in the field of exobiology. The perennial question—Is there life on Mars?—had been given new life itself by *Mariner 9*. Most exobiologists agree that the essential ingredient for the existence of life on another planet is water. Although *Mariner 9* had recorded no current evidence of the present existence of liquid water on Mars, there had apparently been water, and lots of it, on the red planet at some point in its distant past. And there were indications that the Martian ice caps, previously thought to be made only of dry ice (frozen carbon dioxide), might contain some frozen water as well. Perhaps, the ever-hopeful exobiologists speculated, life had emerged and flourished during the red planet's water age; perhaps these life-forms had adapted to the changing conditions, had evolved and survived as life on Earth had. Perhaps they still existed today near the icy poles, like certain lichens that cling to life in Earth's Arctic or Antarctic regions. And if not, they might have left behind evidence that they had in fact once existed.

But all this speculation would remain just that—speculation—until scientists could get their hands on a sample of Martian soil and test it for evidence of organic compounds. NASA did not have the technology to send a scientist to Mars or to build an unmanned craft that could

An impact basin located 50 miles south of the Martian equator served as the touchdown site for the Viking 1 *lander, which arrived on Mars in July 1976. This photograph was taken by the* Viking 1 *orbiter during its daily pass over the area. Scientists hoped that the lander would find evidence of microbial life in the Martian soil.*

retrieve a sample of Martian dirt and bring it back to Earth. What they needed was an unmanned vehicle that could land on Mars, test the soil itself, and transmit the results of the test back to Earth; in effect, a robot scientist. This was the *Viking* Martian lander.

If the *Mariner* probe carried the eyes of earth scientists, then the *Viking* carried their eyes and hands as well as an earthside laboratory. Designed and developed by NASA's Langley Research Center in Virginia, in conjunction with the Martin Marietta Corporation and the Jet Propulsion Laboratory, *Viking* was a minor miracle of space technology. *Viking* had two major components: an orbiter, based on the *Mariner* design and equipped with cameras and other surveying instruments; and a lander, which would separate from the orbiter and attempt a soft touchdown on the Martian surface. The lander weighed 1,300 pounds and was about the size of a small automobile. Bristling with antennas for receiving and transmitting, the *Viking* lander also had a complement of two cameras: stereoscopic "eyes" that would send to Earth three-dimensional color, black-and-white, and infrared images of the Martian surface. *Viking* was an interplanetary weather laboratory as well, equipped with a variety of meteorological and atmospheric sensors. A seismometer would monitor the planet for "Marsquakes." Most remarkable was the *Viking*'s robotic arm, which would scoop up a handful of Martian soil and pour it into the spacecraft's three separate automated laboratory compartments (built by the TRW Corporation of Redondo Beach, California, at a cost of $50 million), where the soil would be analyzed in a number of ways for evidence of the organic compounds that might indicate the presence of life on Mars.

NASA dispatched two of these robotic superscientists to Mars in 1975. The *Viking 1* lander set down in an area known as *Chryse Planitia* (the Plain of Gold) on July 20, 1976. *Viking 2* landed on *Utopia Planitia* (the Utopian Plain), which is located on the other side of the planet,

on September 3, 1976. Both landers went to work immediately and functioned flawlessly. The *Viking 1* lander continued to transmit data until 1982; *Viking 2* remained operative until 1980. Combined orbiter and lander photographs totaled an incredible 51,500 images.

The *Viking* project was a technological triumph for NASA, but it was a disappointment for those who hoped it would turn up evidence of life on Mars. No conclusive evidence was found. Exobiologists were quick to point out that no definitive evidence precluding life on Mars was

Technicians work on the Viking 1 *lander at Kennedy Space Center in Florida. Although the* Viking 1 *would carry no human passengers, it was among the most remarkable of NASA's achievements, for the robotic spacecraft could do many of the things an astronaut might do on Mars.*

found either. Harold Klein, head of *Viking*'s biology team, put it this way: "These are the facts we have. They do not rigorously prove the existence of life on Mars. They do not rigorously exclude the presence of life on Mars. My feeling is, we'll not be able to prove any more until we go back to Mars."

But NASA has not yet returned to Mars. After the *Viking* missions, the space agency turned its attention to the other planets and to deep-space probes. The dogged Soviets, however, had not given up on Mars. In July 1988 they launched two more unmanned Mars probes, *Phobos*

The Martian high plains as seen from the "eyes" of the Viking 1 *lander. The protruding instrument on the right is a meteorology sensor, which measures atmospheric pressure, temperature, wind velocity, and wind direction. The data was then transmitted back to Earth for analysis.*

1 and *Phobos* 2. Named after one of the two moons of Mars (Phobos and Deimos), the objective of these probes was to orbit Mars and to set a lander down on Phobos. But *Phobos 1* was given an erroneous radio command by a flight controller and as a result was irretrievably lost in space. *Phobos 2* fared a little better, completing an aerial survey of Mars and Phobos, but it too failed to place a lander on the moon's surface.

Despite the Soviets' troubles, by the time the faithful *Viking 1* stopped transmitting from Mars in November 1982, the red planet was no longer the mysterious orb it had been down through the ages. Scientists now knew more about Mars than they knew about any other planet in the solar system except Earth. The question of what Mars is like could finally be answered with a certain authority, and the astronauts or cosmonauts who eventually attempt to go to Mars will know quite a bit about their destination.

Mars is the fourth planet from the sun. Its mean distance from the sun is 141 million miles. Like the other planets in our solar system, Mars is fixed in an elliptical orbit around the sun. It takes Mars 687 days to orbit the sun once; thus a Mars year is almost as long as 2 Earth years. Like Earth, Mars rotates on its axis, completing one rotation every 24 hours, 37 minutes, and 22 seconds, and thus a Mars day is about the same in duration as an Earth day. And like Earth, Mars is tilted on its axis at an angle of about 23 degrees and therefore has 4 seasons every year. Mars is roughly 4,200 miles in diameter, about half the size of Earth. Because of its relatively low mass, Mars has a much weaker gravity than Earth. A human on Mars would weigh only 38 percent of his normal Earth weight.

Mars has two moons, appropriately named after the two consorts of the Roman god Mars—Phobos (fear) and Deimos (panic). Deimos, the outer moon, orbits Mars once every 30 hours; Phobos, the inner moon, once every 7 hours. They are dark objects of an irregular shape, and

they are tiny. Phobos, at its widest point, has a diameter
of 17 miles; Deimos has a 10 mile diameter at its widest
point (Earth's moon, in comparison, has a diameter of
2,160 miles). For an astronaut or a Martian on Mars,
Deimos would appear as a tiny point of light moving slowly
(it takes about 60 hours from horizon to horizon) from

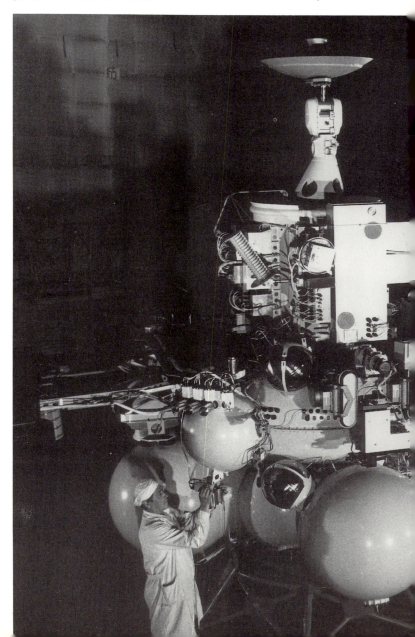

east to west across the sky. Phobos, on the other hand, would appear as a much larger orb, rising in the west and setting in the east in about four hours.

Visitors observing the planet from an orbiting spacecraft would see polar regions much like Earth's Arctic and Antarctic circles. Mars has large polar ice caps that expand

Soviet technicians work on a full-size replica of their Mars Phobos *probes.* Phobos 1 *and* Phobos 2 *were launched in July 1988. Both probes failed—a disastrous turn of events for the Soviets' ambitious Mars program.*

in the winter and recede in the summer. The ice at the Martian poles is mostly frozen carbon dioxide, but the caps also contain some frozen water as well. Comparative planetologists also suspect that, as on Earth, there are extensive layers of permafrost beneath the Martian polar caps and that these frozen water deposits are connected in some way to the massive flooding that once inundated much of the planet. The presence of water on Mars, albeit frozen, also has significant ramifications for exobiologists and for possible permanent settlement of the planet by humans.

Passing over the southern hemisphere in their spacecraft, Mars explorers would see terrain much like the Apollo astronauts encountered on Earth's moon: ancient, desolate, heavily cratered deserts, untroubled for billions of years by water flow or any geologic or volcanic activity. Flying over the northern hemisphere, however, an awesome landscape would come into view, and observers would be startled to see a topography completely unlike the pocked plains of the south. The surface of the northern hemisphere appears to be the tortured result of immense forces at work. There are what appear to be extensive networks of rivers and their tributaries and drainage systems; they are all waterless now, but apparently, at one time in the distant past, they brimmed over with roaring floodwaters. Many planetologists believe that the great Martian flood was caused by a sudden, rapid release of subsurface water deposits like the permafrost locked beneath the ice caps. It will be the task of future pioneer geologists to solve the riddle of the great flood of Mars. Perhaps there was a Martian Noah.

Also visible to orbiting space travelers would be the great canyons of Mars. The largest of these is a canyon so gigantic that it could easily swallow Earth's Grand Canyon. This is *Valles Marineris*, a stunning, 2,800-mile-long gash that runs alongside the equator. *Valles Marineris* is as much as 150 miles long and 3 miles deep. Even more

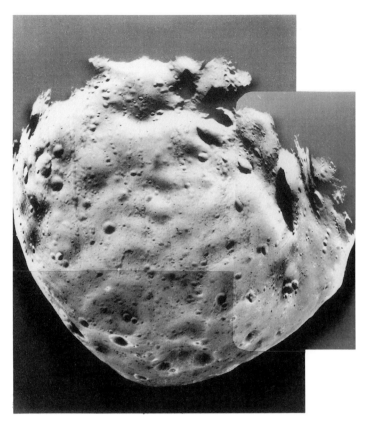

Phobos, one of the two moons of Mars, in a photographic mosaic made up of pictures taken by the Viking 1 orbiter. A tiny moon, Phobos is only about 13 miles across and 11 miles from top to bottom. Its gravity is so weak that a person with a strong arm—perhaps a major-league baseball player—standing on its surface could throw a baseball into orbit.

impressive are the Martian volcanos that mottle the surface of the northern hemisphere. Clustered along a massive bulge in the Martian crust called the Tharsis ridge, these volcanos dwarf anything and everything on Earth. The largest is *Olympus Mons*; no other volcano or mountain in the solar system is nearly as big. *Olympus Mons* is 90,000 feet high and 300 miles across at its base. Its mouth is 50 miles wide and at least 10,000 feet deep.

Having orbited Mars, the spacecraft would attempt a landing—that is, if its passengers were not scared off by *Olympus Mons* and if one of the planet's fierce, global dust storms was not sweeping the surface. Most likely, the touchdown would be made on one of the vast, level Martian plains. Then, the explorers would prepare to venture

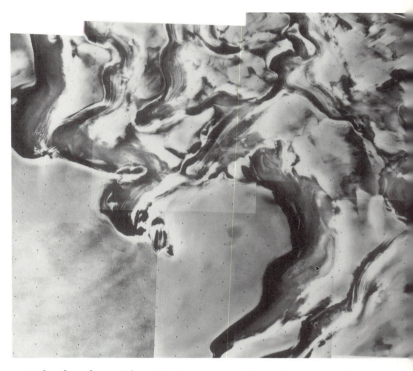

outside the ship. The Martian atmosphere is extremely thin. It is 95 percent carbon dioxide; the other 5 percent is made up of oxygen, nitrogen, and argon, along with traces of water vapor, carbon monoxide, neon, krypton, and xenon. And Mars is cold. At the equator, the warmest location on Mars, temperatures range from a high of 0 degrees Fahrenheit to a low of -150 degrees Fahrenheit. The low temperatures, low oxygen content, and low atmospheric pressure as well as the deadly radiation that constantly beats down on the planet's surface would require a surface explorer to wear a pressure suit much like the suits the Apollo moon walkers wore. After stepping out of the spacecraft and onto the high plains of Mars, pressure-suited earthlings would find themselves in a dusty, rust-colored landscape under a weird, salmon pink sky. Even up close, Mars is essentially a red planet (the sands of Mars are believed to be partly made up of iron

As the Viking 2 *orbiter passed over the north pole of Mars, it photographed these curious features. Planetologists believe that the semitranslucent, layered formations of dry ice are shaped by high winds at the poles.*

deposits that have rusted, which accounts for the redness of the planet).

Explorers from Earth know what to expect on this new world. Not great canals; not the ruined cities of lost Martian civilizations; not Martians or monsters or little green men; but rather barren, red deserts continually bombarded by ultraviolet rays from the sun; blinding, month-long global dust blizzards; dry riverbeds; volcanos and lava fields; and sub-subzero temperatures. Mars, in short, is a brutal place, an airless, waterless, freezing, irradiated, dust-choked desert; a cross between Antarctica and Death Valley. Why would anyone want to go there? One would think that once the romantic mystery of Lowell's Mars had been replaced—thanks mostly to the *Mariner* and *Viking* probes—by these harsh facts, humans would not be so eager to go there. And yet, as the millenium draws closer, so too does Mars.

Forward to Mars

Although the objectives of NASA's manned space program have been somewhat murky since Project Apollo ended in 1972, there is no question about the ultimate outer-space goal of the Soviet government. Forward to Mars has been the official slogan of the Soviet space agency since the early seventies. After conceding the moon race to NASA following the circumlunar flight of *Apollo 8* in 1968 and after finishing second best in the unmanned Mars race as well, the Soviets focused their attention on the long-range objective of putting a cosmonaut on the red planet. Toward this end they have made considerable progress, especially in one of the more crucial areas of potential interplanetary spaceflight. A successful Mars mission depends as much on physiological issues as it does on technological ones. And the key physiological question, the one upon which the entire proposition hinges, is this: How will the human physique react to an extended spaceflight of at least a year and perhaps more than two years?

The Soviet Union has addressed this question—and many others—through an ongoing space station program that began in the late sixties. Construction of *Salyut 1*, the first-ever manned space station, began in 1969. The *Salyut* was about 80 feet long from end to end and had 3 cylindrical compartments. The transfer compartment on the forward end of the space station functioned as a docking

Soyuz TM-7 blasts off from a launchpad at Baikonur Cosmodrome in the Soviet republic of Kazakhstan, November 26, 1988. The Soyuz *will carry three cosmonauts—two Soviets and one Frenchman—to the* Mir *space station, where they will join the three inhabitants of the* Mir *to conduct biological and technological research.*

adapter and an airlock entrance-and-exit tunnel for cosmonauts. (In order to occupy the *Salyut*, which would be launched into orbit unmanned, cosmonauts in a separately launched *Soyuz* spacecraft would rendezvous and dock with the station and then enter through the transfer compartment.) The main section of the *Salyut* was the living and working quarters, where the cosmonauts would eat,

In March 1981, a life-size replica of the Soviet "space train"— docked Progress *(left),* Salyut *(center), and* Soyuz *(right) spacecraft—was put on public display in Moscow to mark the 20th anniversary of cosmonaut Yury Gagarin's historic flight. The exhibit also testified to the Soviets' progress in developing and perfecting space station technology.*

exercise, sleep, and carry out various experiments, tests, and other duties. At the rear of the station was a service module containing the *Salyut's* propulsion system.

Although the Soviets are now considered to have an undisputed edge over the United States in space station technology and know-how, their *Salyut* orbital habitats did not have an auspicious beginning. *Salyut 1* was placed (unmanned) into a low Earth orbit on April 19, 1971, by a *Proton* booster rocket. On April 24, three cosmonauts in a *Soyuz* spacecraft rendezvoused successfully with the space station. However, docking could not be completed because of a malfunction in the coupling apparatus of the *Soyuz*, and the cosmonauts returned to Earth without having entered the space station. Six weeks later, a second team of cosmonauts succeeded in occupying the space station. The crew—Georgy Dobrovolsky, Vladislav Volkov, and Viktor Patsayev—inhabited the *Salyut* for 24 days, a new space-endurance record. On June 29, the men returned to the *Soyuz* and undocked from the space station; on June 30 they executed a seemingly routine reentry and touchdown. But the technicians who opened the hatch on the *Soyuz* encountered a strange scene—the three cosmonauts appeared to be sound asleep in the cockpit. Closer examination revealed that Dobrovolsky, Volkov, and Patsayev were dead, killed by a sudden, accidental loss of cabin pressure during their descent to Earth.

The death of the three *Soyuz* cosmonauts was, up to that point, the worst in-flight accident in the history of space exploration. It is a testimony to the resilience of the Soviet space agency (and to the courage of the cosmonaut corps as well) that their plans and objectives were not undermined by the shock waves that swept through the agency's infrastructure as a result of the tragedy. Instead, with grim, stubborn determination, the Soviets pressed on with their plans. Between 1971 and 1977, the Soviets launched 14 *Salyut*-related missions and numerous missions involving the *Soyuz Ferry*, a spacecraft developed to shuttle cosmonauts to and from the *Salyuts*. Initially, failure followed upon failure, and although there were no more fatalities, there were no notable successes involving the space stations until 1973.

Finally, there was a breakthrough. On June 24, 1973, *Salyut* 3 was launched into orbit. *Salyut* 3 was different from the original *Salyut*. The new space station consisted of two rather than three cylindrical compartments. The living section, as it was called, was equipped with four portholes, two fold-out beds, a table, a little library, a tape recorder, a water tank, a toilet, a shower, and a chess set. On July 5, cosmonauts Pavel Popovich and Yurity Artyukhin docked their *Soyuz* with *Salyut* 3 and safely transferred to the space station. They remained at the station for 16 days and returned to Earth on July 19.

On December 26, 1974, *Salyut 4*, a modified version of *Salyut 1*, was put into Earth orbit. Two weeks later it was entered by another two-man crew, who discovered a Wipe Your Feet sign in the airlock as they crossed into the station, proving that the technicians at the Baikonur Cosmodrome (the massive launch center in the remote republic of Kazakhstan) still had a sense of humor. The cosmonauts occupied the space station for 29 days before returning to Earth. In May 1975, two more cosmonauts arrived at *Salyut 4*; they stayed for 63 days, the longest occupation of a first-generation Soviet space station.

From 1977 to 1985, the Soviets carried out their second-generation *Salyut* program. The second-generation space stations were different from their predecessors in two important ways: They could be resupplied in orbit while the crew remained on board, which allowed the Soviets to keep a space station operating and manned indefinitely by rotating crews; and they could be almost doubled in size through the addition of the new *Star* module, which was launched separately and attached to the *Salyut* in orbit.

The second generation *Salyut* program was the most successful and productive Soviet outer-space endeavor since their historic *Vostok* spacecraft first carried a human into orbit. As far as manned mission-to-Mars research and development is concerned, it was the most important program to date completed by either superpower. Sixty-two *Salyut*-related missions were undertaken between 1977 and 1985. During this effort, invaluable advances in interior and exterior space-station support systems were made. Atmosphere-regeneration, water-recovery, and solar-energy systems were tested and improved. Extravehicular repair techniques were mastered by the cosmonauts. And the new, robotic *Progress* cargo-transport spacecraft and *Soyuz T* cosmonaut ferry were also successfully deployed and utilized during the second-generation period.

The most important advances made by the Soviets during this time concerned manned outer-space endurance records. New records were continually set and then shattered by *Salyut* cosmonauts. The initial second-generation crew inhabited *Salyut 6* for 96 days in 1977–78. In 1982, *Salyut 7* was occupied for 211 days and in 1984 for 237 days. By the time the third-generation *Mir* space station was first sent aloft in 1986, the Soviets were making plans

The crew of the ill-fated Soyuz 11—*test engineer Viktor Patsayev (left), mission commander Georgy Dobrovolsky (center), and flight engineer Vladislav Volkov—pose for a photograph at the Gagarin Training Center at Baikonur. The three cosmonauts were killed during reentry on June 30, 1971.*

for year-long and even 30-month cosmonaut missions. Clearly the Soviets were gaining expertise and confidence in designing, launching, and maintaining their space stations, and any doubts left over from the early *Salyut 1* days had finally dissipated. And with each new endurance

record, with each additional day spent aboard a space station, the Soviets were a little closer to Mars.

The Soviets were making great strides in other Mars-related areas as well. In May 1987, they launched their first *Energia* super booster. The *Energia* is a workhorse

NASA's Skylab space station in Earth orbit. Skylab was launched in May 1973 and was inhabited by 3 successive astronaut crews for a total of 171 days and 13 hours. Abandoned in early 1974, the space station eventually fell back to Earth. Breaking up as it plummeted through the atmosphere, most of Skylab landed in the Indian Ocean and the Australian outback.

The space shuttle Discovery's *mechanical arm, or remote manipulator system, deploys the Hubble Space Telescope, which was carried into space in the shuttle's cargo bay in April 1990. The space shuttle's manipulator has been an invaluable tool for NASA and will be even more so in the future, especially in regard to the building and maintenance of space stations.*

rocket. Versatile and powerful, the *Energia* can carry a variety of heavy payloads, including space station components and the Soviet space shuttle *Boran*. The *Energia* will play a crucial role in any Soviet manned mission to Mars. It also gives the Soviets the booster capability needed to build a large, permanent space station (tentatively called *Cosmograd*) that might host a population of as many as 100 people, and also a permanent outpost on the moon.

What was NASA doing while the Soviets were in the process of permanently occupying Earth-orbit space? The last manned Apollo flight took place in December 1972. Project Apollo was a triumph for NASA, but after the

exhilaration of the manned lunar program wore off, ennui
set in. Neil Armstrong's walk on the moon was a tough
act to follow. The public's attitude toward space exploration cooled considerably, and Congress sharply reduced
funding to NASA. President Richard Nixon, hoping to
provide a new focus for American manned space exploration (and well aware of the Soviet's space station program), set in motion two new projects. The first was the
Skylab space station project. *Skylab*, Nixon hoped, would
be the American reply to the Soviets' *Salyut*. *Skylab* was
a self-contained habitat propelled into earth orbit by the
massive *Saturn 5* rocket. Astronauts launched separately
in a conventional *Apollo* command module would dock
with and then occupy *Skylab*. The station itself was spa-
cious compared to the original *Salyuts*; it had 10,000 cubic
feet of space and 2 compartments—a workshop and a living
area. NASA hoped that *Skylab* would be the start of interplanetary research and development, the foundation for
an eventual mission to Mars. But *Skylab* was plagued by
technical failures and mishaps from the start, and in the
end it fell far short of the Soviet space station accomplishments, both literally and figuratively. Only three manned
missions were undertaken, from May 1973 to February
1974. The third mission was the longest, lasting 84 days.
Although the *Skylab* project had yielded valuable results,
a wary Congress refused to provide further funding, and
NASA's space station project was over, at least for the time
being. The abandoned *Skylab* was left in a decaying orbit,
and it fell ingloriously to Earth, amid much dubious publicity, in July 1979. NASA turned its attention to the space
shuttle.

The space shuttle project would be NASA's most important since Apollo. The shuttle had its origins back in
the post-Apollo Nixon years; in a way, it actually grew out
of the doomed *Skylab* project. The space shuttle was initially proposed as an economical way to service *Skylab* and
future space stations. The cost of sending a conventional

rocket to *Skylab* was extremely high—$120 million per launch. A reusable space shuttle might service an Earth-orbit station for much less. And, NASA argued, the space shuttle was a multipurpose vehicle. It could be used for many different tasks, including scientific research and the deployment of various military, weather, and commercial satellites.

Congress and President Nixon were sold on the concept of the space shuttle, and in 1972, Nixon approved a $5.5 billion budget for shuttle research and development. When *Skylab* was scrapped and plans for other space stations were put on indefinite hold, NASA focused its resources on the shuttle, believing it to be the linchpin of all future space exploration—including interplanetary travel. The American public responded favorably to the space shuttle idea as well. They had never quite gotten behind *Skylab*, which had always seemed somewhat pedestrian and aimless compared to Project Apollo. The space shuttle, on the other hand, provided the United States with a spacecraft that actually did something and a space program that was once again leading somewhere.

Essentially, the space shuttle is a jetlinerlike craft, called an orbiter, that can fly in outer space and then return to Earth and land like a conventional jet airplane. The shuttle is carried into space by two simple booster rockets; once it is in orbit, the boosters are jettisoned and the shuttle becomes a maneuverable spacecraft piloted by an astronaut. When the orbital mission is over, the pilot will glide the spacecraft back to Earth and land it on a runway. In this manner, the shuttle can be used repeatedly, like any conventional aircraft.

The orbiter itself is divided into two main sections—the forward crew cabin and the cargo bay. The crew cabin consists of an upper deck, or flight deck, from which the pilot and copilot fly the shuttle; behind them are two additional seats. There are 10 windows in this area, 6 located in front of the pilots, 2 overhead, and 2 at the rear overlooking the cargo bay. A ladder extends through a hole in the flight deck floor to the lower deck where three more crew members or passengers might sit. The lower deck also contains the sleeping quarters, the kitchen, the bathroom, and additional space. Leading out of the lower deck is a tunnel and air lock connecting the crew cabin with the cargo area.

Most of the space in the shuttle's fuselage is taken up by the cargo bay, or payload bay. The cargo area is used

The space shuttle Columbia, *riding its booster rockets, blasts off from the Kennedy Space Center on April 12, 1981. The* Columbia, *piloted by astronauts John Young and Bob Crippen, spent 54 hours in Earth orbit during this first outer-space test flight.*

*The crew members of space
shuttle mission 51-L on their way
to the launchpad at Kennedy
Space Center, where they will
board the* Challenger *and prepare
for lift-off, on January 28, 1986.
From front to back are Francis
R. Scobee, Judith A. Resnik,
Ronald E. McNair, Michael J.
Smith, Christa McAuliffe,
Ellison Onizuka, and
Gregory B. Jarvis.*

primarily for carrying satellites and other devices such as
a portable science laboratory known as *Spacelab* (designed
by the European Space Agency) or the Hubble Space Telescope. When the crew must deploy or retrieve such equipment, the bay's giant doors are opened outward onto space.
(The doors serve a dual purpose; they are lined with large
solar panels that function as an energy source for the shuttle while in orbit.) Located inside the bay is one of the
shuttle's most remarkable features—a huge mechanical

arm that can grab objects, either releasing them into orbit or picking them out of space as they hover near the shuttle. The manipulator can be operated not only from inside the cargo bay but also from inside the forward crew cabin.

The public got its first glimpse of the new spacecraft in action in February 1977 when astronauts Fred Haise and Gordon Fullerton took the shuttle *Enterprise* on a test run. The *Enterprise* rode piggyback on a specially equipped Boeing 747 to an altitude of 25,000 feet and then broke away. Escorted by an air force fighter jet, the *Enterprise* glided safely back to Earth. The *Enterprise* made four more trial flights, and by 1981, NASA was ready for the shuttle's first outer-space journey.

The first orbital mission was flown by the shuttle *Columbia* in April 1981 and lasted for two days. Although the mission was a relative success, pilot John Young and copilot Robert Crippen sweated out some frightening moments in orbit when they noticed that several heat-resistant tiles were missing from the wing area. Thirty thousand silica tiles cover the outside of the shuttle; without them the spacecraft will burn up upon reentering the Earth's atmosphere. Flight controllers and the two astronauts feared that a "zipper effect"—the progressive peeling away of the tiles—might be occurring. Fortunately this was not the case, and Young and Crippen brought the *Columbia* to a picture-perfect three-point landing at Edwards Air Force Base in California's Mojave Desert.

Although the mission was declared a tremendous success by NASA, the heat-tile problem turned out to be the first incident in a disturbing trend of increasingly serious— and dangerous—problems afflicting NASA's fleet of shuttles. This trend culminated in the infamous *Challenger* disaster. On January 28, 1986, the space shuttle *Challenger* exploded just 73 seconds into a planned 6-day orbital mission. All seven crew members were killed. It was by far the worst catastrophe in the history of manned spaceflight.

Predictably, the shuttle program was suspended while Congress and NASA launched inquiries. While pieces of the *Challenger*—including the crew cabin, which contained the remains of the seven dead astronauts—were raised from the ocean floor, investigators were discovering that the tragedy was the result of a combination of factors, including faulty parts, human error, and freezing weather. The nation was horrified to learn that the accident could have been prevented and that safety had been sacrificed in the interests of keeping the shuttle program on schedule and within its budget.

NASA has struggled to recover its balance in the wake of the *Challenger* explosion. In September 1988 the orbiter *Discovery* was launched, signaling the resumption of the space shuttle project. But the shuttle continues to be a problematic and controversial spacecraft, suffering from repeated launch delays and postponements caused by nagging fuel tank and booster flaws. In-flight difficulties continue as well. In June 1991, during a nine-day mission, the shuttle *Columbia*'s cargo-bay doors refused to close. Although the malfunction was eventually corrected, it was potentially disastrous—if the astronauts had attempted reentry with the doors open, the spacecraft would have burned up. Nevertheless, NASA, much like the Soviet agency, has persevered in times of crisis. The shuttle fleet has slowly expanded, and its work load has increased. Significantly, the space shuttle has already played an important role in NASA's steadily growing interest in a manned Mars expedition. The shuttles have completed numerous missions involving scientific research directly related to the question of interplanetary spaceflight. The same shuttle that developed a problem with its cargo-bay doors, for example, carried physician-astronauts who were engaged in research into the effects of long-term weightlessness on the human cardiovascular system. As the nineties progress and momentum for a manned mission to Mars grows in the United States—and the technological foundation for such a mission is built—the shuttle fleet, as well as the Soviet space stations and *Energia* rocket, will fulfill its promise. Perhaps, decades or centuries from now, the three cosmonauts killed in the *Soyuz* tragedy and the seven astronauts killed in the *Challenger* disaster will be remembered as the first martyrs in humanity's long march to Mars.

A section of the destroyed space shuttle Challenger *is lowered into an abandoned Minuteman missile silo at Cape Canaveral, Florida. Two vacant silos serve as the final resting place for the remains of the* Challenger.

How?

As the millennium approaches, the call for a manned mission to Mars can be heard from many quarters, most loudly from the United States and the Soviet Union, the two premier outer-space, as well as terrestrial, powers. It seems almost inevitable that such a mission will take place sometime in the early decades of the 21st century. Serious consideration is now being given to the logistics of such a journey. One of the questions being asked is, of course, How?

Mars, at its closest approach, is a little less than 35 million miles away from Earth. (The elliptical orbit of Mars brings it to within 35 million miles of Earth about once every 26 months. Mars is about 63 million miles away from Earth at its farthest approach.) It is estimated that a spacecraft fully manned, equipped, and provisioned for the passage to Mars might weigh as much as 1 million pounds (500 tons). Engineers are faced with the task of figuring out how to propel such a heavy payload up and out of Earth's atmosphere and then through interplanetary space for 35 million miles or so.

The most powerful rocket currently in use is the Soviet *Energia*, which can lift, at most, a payload of about 230 tons into Earth orbit. The most powerful expendable American booster, the *Titan 4*, can lift only about 25 tons.

The Soviet multipurpose booster Energia *can be used to piggyback into orbit the* Boran *space shuttle, which is almost identical to NASA's space shuttle. The versatile* Energia, *first launched in May 1987, can also propel a variety of payloads into space, and it will play a major role in the construction of extensive Earth-orbit space stations and perhaps a colony on the moon.*

The 500-ton Mars spacecraft, therefore, will have to be launched into orbit piece by piece and then assembled by astronauts or cosmonauts at a space station. This might require numerous launches of not only a booster such as the *Energia,* but numerous launches of shuttle-type spacecraft as well. The U.S. shuttle fleet or the Soviet shuttle *Buran* or the *Soyuz Ferry* that services the *Mir* space station could carry workers and supplies to and from the in-orbit space station, which would steadily expand as the project continued, becoming a manufacturing plant in outer space.

The space station would have to contain living units, warehouses, work areas, and tank farms (large stores of rocket propellant) and would undoubtedly be an extremely hazardous place. As the station orbited Earth, men and women would be required to engage in assembly activities involving the use of heavy machinery, volatile materials, and large, free-floating pieces of equipment. Mechanics and engineers might frequently be called upon to perform extravehicular assembly or repair duties. Accidents, injuries, and perhaps even fatalities would be most likely to occur during this phase of the project.

The multiple launches from Earth of heavy payloads and the need for a separate, interplanetary propulsion system to power the spacecraft from Earth orbit to Mars and back again will most likely require vast amounts of cryogenic (supercooled) rocket fuels like the propellants used for the Apollo missions—mostly kerosene, liquid hydrogen, and liquid oxygen. But other possibilities are being explored. Various governmental and private agencies in the United States, under the auspices of the Pentagon, are currently investigating a new kind of nuclear reactor—called a particle bed reactor—intended for use in large, and as yet unbuilt, booster rockets. Code-named "Timberwind," the classified project reportedly concerns the development of a small nuclear reactor that will power a

(continued on page 73)

Resolution on Mars

Planetary probe Viking 1 *took this photograph of Mars during its first approach in July 1976.*

No other celestial body has been the subject of such speculation or the source of such mystery. It was the *redness* of the planet that first drew the attention of humans—the bloody color set it apart from all the other stars and planets that shimmered in the night sky. The advent of telescopes allowed the earthbound to get a closer look. But some observers, such as the fantasy-prone Percival Lowell, looked for too long and saw on the face of the planet such things as canals, pyramids, giant messages written in Hebrew, and strange humanoid faces. The mystery of Mars deepened, for the telescopes of the day could not bring human eyes close enough to resolve the planet's riddles. But writers, painters, and filmmakers could, and imagination filled in where science left off. Finally, beginning in 1966, NASA's unmanned *Mariner* and *Viking* probes orbited and then landed on Mars. Thousands of photographs were taken—including those on the following pages—and people could finally see what the red planet actually looks like. The artwork also included on the following pages, however, shows that the human imagination remains a step ahead of the capabilities of even the most advanced technology.

A Viking's *eye view of the Utopian Plain on the surface of Mars. Part of the* Viking 2 *lander can be seen in the lower right corner.*

As it passed over the northern hemisphere of Mars, Viking 1 *photographed enormous Valles Marineris, a canyon 2,500 miles long, 100 miles wide, and 3 miles deep.*

Martian sunset, photographed by Viking 1.

Olympus Mons, the colossal Martian volcano, photographed by the Viking 1 orbiter. Olympus Mons is about the size of Missouri.

Mars up close. Oxidized metals in the rocks and soil give the planet its reddish color.

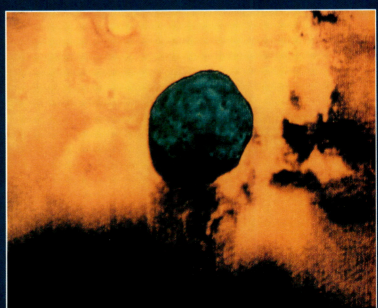

Phobos, one of the two tiny moons of Mars, passes in front of the mother planet. First sighted by astronomer Asaph Hall in 1877, Phobos is 17 miles in diameter at its widest point.

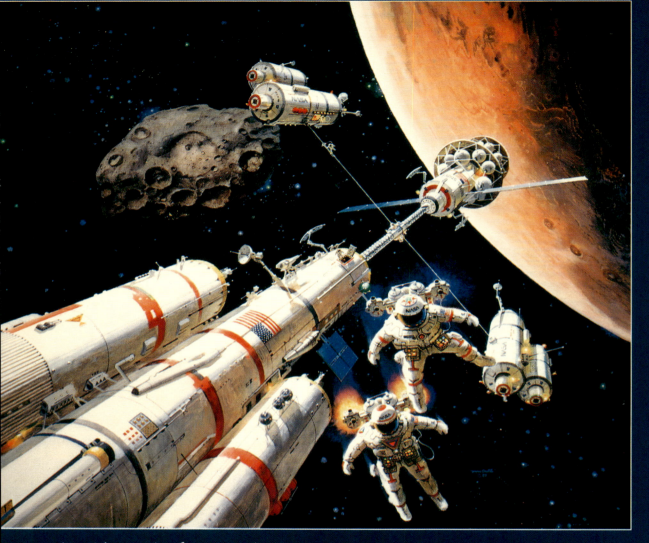

*An artist's conception of a transportation
depot in Mars orbit. The depot allows
astronauts to engage in resource mining on
Phobos; it also serves as a docking port
and way station for arriving and departing
spacecraft and their passengers.*

A possible scene from Mars's future: In this artist's conception of Martian exploration, astronauts undertake a sunrise reconnaissance at Valles Marineris.

A cutaway view of a proposed space habitat for 10,000 people. The habitat's population, as well as its trees, crops, streams, and homes, is protected from solar and cosmic radiation by a spherical shell made of material mined from the moon. The inner surface of the sphere, nearly a mile in circumference, rotates to provide gravity by centrifugal force.

*After Mars, what next? Perhaps an expedition to Jupiter, whose
many moons have attracted the attention of science fiction writers
and planetologists alike. In this photograph, Jupiter (upper right) is
accompanied by four of its moons, including Io (upper left),
Europa (center), Ganymede (lower left), and Callisto.*

(continued from page 64)
new class of superboosters. Revolutionary power sources such as matter-antimatter and solar-thermal rocket engines are also being investigated for use as interplanetary propulsion.

Once assembly of the Mars spacecraft is completed, the crew will be brought from Earth on a shuttle; they will board the newly assembled interplanetary vessel, which will then be fueled, powered up, and launched—without having to battle Earth's atmosphere and gravity—toward Mars. (In the tradition of maritime exploration, some mission-to-Mars advocates are calling for the use of two spacecraft in the expedition, in case one of them malfunctions or becomes disabled.)

What will the first manned interplanetary spacecraft be like? It will be big, first of all; big enough to carry a crew of at least 4 and perhaps as many as 10 or 12, as well as the required tonnage of supplies and equipment. It will look nothing like the streamlined rocket ships, command modules, or space shuttles of the 20th century; instead, it will more likely be an asymmetrical conglomeration of different components, each having a separate function. (The first Mars craft might closely resemble the Soviet *Mir* space station; there is some speculation that the Soviets have plans to use a modified *Mir* as an interplanetary vessel.)

This cluster of interconnected modules and components—the mother ship—might include a command-and-control station; a habitation module for eating, sleeping, exercise, and recreation; a laboratory or workplace module; large fuel and water tanks; aeroshells (large, convex protective shields for entry into the Martian atmosphere); and a Mars landing vehicle that will separate from the mother ship once Mars orbit is achieved, land on the planet's surface, and eventually return the astronauts or cosmonauts to the mother ship for the long trip home. The entire cluster will be pushed along by a liquid-fuel or perhaps nuclear propulsion system. Its computers, communications systems, and life-support systems might be powered by conventional batteries, fuel cells that combine hydrogen and oxygen to produce electricity, solar energy, or a combination of the three. (A nuclear-electrical power source is possible as well. The Soviets are reportedly developing

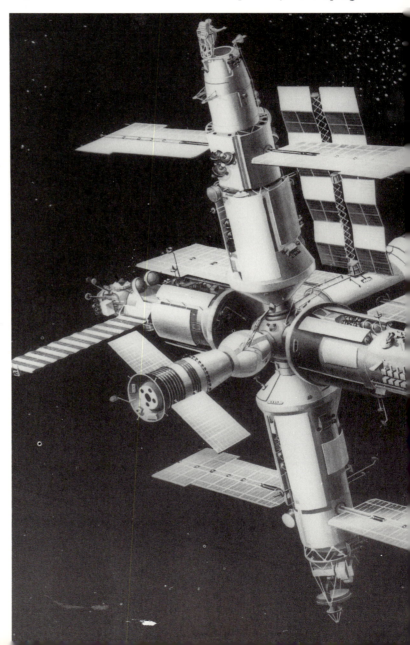

a small, outer-space nuclear power plant called Topaz, and NASA has been studying nuclear submarines for possible interplanetary applications.)

Mother ship is an especially appropriate term for the vehicle that will take humans to Mars and return them safely to Earth. The mother ship will function not only

An artist's conception of the expanded Mir *space station. For scale, note the cosmonauts engaged in exterior maintenance. The Soviets have been adding various habitation, research, and storage modules to* Mir *since 1987, and some observers believe that the completed* Mir *will be utilized as a Mars vessel.*

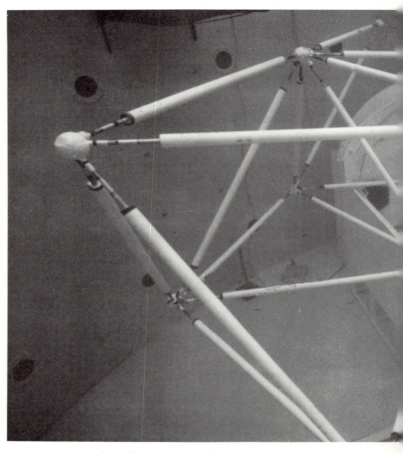

as a transporter but also as a provider, nurturer, and protector—a life-sustaining womb for the men and woman who dare to venture so far from their natural environment for so long. Various estimates—depending on the trajectory and speed of the spacecraft and on the time spent in Mars orbit and on the surface—are given for the duration of a voyage to Mars and back. It could take 18 months round trip or 3 years. The ship will have to provide its passengers with food, water, and oxygen for that length of time. The solid food—perhaps as much as two tons—will have to be hauled along in storage. Ideally, a Mars ship will have a closed environmental life-support system that

Astronauts practice extravehicular construction and repair in a massive water tank, known as the Neutral Buoyance Simulator, at the Marshall Space Flight Center in Huntsville, Alabama. The underwater environment, which approximates the zero gravity of outer space, allows astronauts to develop and refine the skills— as well as the materials—needed to build and maintain space stations.

will recycle oxygen and water. A closed life-support system will also be indispensable to any Mars settlements established by humans. The Soviets have done considerable delving into this question on their *Mir* space station. NASA has lagged far behind but is starting to catch up, and certain private concerns in America and other countries have been doing valuable research into closed life-support systems through the use of terrestrial biospheres. (A biosphere is an enclosed, self-sustaining ecosystem.)

Along with sustenance, the mother ship will have to be equipped with certain features that will protect its passengers from some of the unique hazards of interplanetary travel (in addition to the more familiar hazards of orbital or translunar spaceflight such as loss of cabin pressure, fire, fuel-tank leaks and explosions, and micrometeoroids—tiny, high-velocity particles that can punch a hole in a spacecraft, space suit, or space traveler). Recycled air and water must be purified and a virtually sterile environment must be maintained to prevent bacterial infections in the crew. The mother ship must also provide protection from deep-space radiation if the crew is to survive the journey. Without the shield of the earth's atmosphere and magnetic field, a Mars craft in interplanetary space will be bombarded by radiation of both solar and intergalactic origin. Most deadly for the crew are the powerful waves of energy emitted by the sun during solar flares (brief periods of intense solar activity). The hull of the mother ship must be made of, or reinforced by, substances that will protect the crew from these potentially fatal rays.

What route might our spacecraft take to Mars? One might think that the best route would be the most direct— a straight line from Earth to Mars. But in determining the best Earth-to-Mars trajectory, many variables come into play. For example, both Mars and Earth are constantly in motion, each moving at a different speed in its orbit around the sun, so there is no simple straight-line route. The sun and some of the planets will exert a gravitational influence on an interplanetary spacecraft—an influence that might be either a help or a hindrance. And there are fuel, food, and time considerations as well. Some trajectories will be more economical as far as fuel consumption is concerned but will take much longer and therefore require larger stores of food and water. Less travel time but more fuel might be required by another, shorter trajectory. The debate over this issue is hot; the very nature of the journey will be determined by the Earth-to-Mars trajectory chosen. Will the trip to Mars be an all-out, fuel-consumptive sprint, an Apollo-like push to get there and back as fast as possible? Will it be a more economical (as far as fuel is concerned) and time-consuming voyage, a journey of scientific exploration rather than a race? Or will it be an evolutionary process, carried out step by step over many decades and resulting ultimately in a permanent manned outpost on Mars?

Many experts advocate a sprint mission, much like NASA's Project Apollo, which was in essence a concentrated effort to put a man on the moon as quickly and as cheaply as possible. One sprint scenario calls for sending two spacecraft to Mars. An unmanned cargo ship, containing food and fuel for the journey home, would be sent ahead via a slow trajectory that would require a minimum amount of fuel. The cargo ship would arrive in Mars orbit months ahead of the manned ship. The manned ship, free of the weight of the return fuel and food supply, would get to Mars as quickly as possible via a fast trajectory. The manned craft would then rendezvous with the cargo craft in Mars orbit. In this manner, the entire round trip for the crew—including exploration of the planet—might take only 15 months.

Another sprint scenario has been suggested by astronaut-writer Michael Collins, command-module pilot for the historic *Apollo 11* mission and author of several exceptionally lucid books on space exploration. In his book *Mission to Mars*, Collins proposes "using the gravitational field of Venus as a slingshot to speed a spacecraft on its way to Mars. Remember that Venus is closer to the Sun than Earth, while Mars is farther away. Aiming at Venus while intending to end up at Mars may seem like going off in exactly the wrong direction, but orbital mechanics, involving intricate curved paths of varying speeds, is a deceptive science. It's sort of like ski jumping: the best way to soar high is to get up a good head of steam going downhill." By using Venus as a ski ramp, Collins believes a spacecraft could get to Mars in 11 months with reduced

energy and fuel requirements. Collins and his fellow sprint
proponents believe that the first manned mission to Mars
could be accomplished before the year 2010.

At the other end of the mission-to-Mars spectrum are
those who are calling for a gradual, step by step, evolutionary approach to the red planet. Decrying a sprint to
Mars as a mere stunt, the conservatives advocate taking a
slower, safer road. The first step along the way would be
the building and maintaining of a large and complex space
station in Earth orbit; something like the Soviets' proposed
orbital "city," Cosmograd. Next, using the space station
as a staging area, a permanent colony on the moon would
be established. The moon colony would then serve as a

staging area for not one but rather a continuing series of manned journeys to Mars, which would allow a permanent outpost on Mars to be established, maintained, and then expanded upon, much like the *Mir* space station. This approach to Mars would obviously require a much longer timetable than a sprint scenario; if the project began in the year 2000, it would be another 30 or 40 years at the very least before the first manned ship reached Mars. But proponents of the Earth-to-moon-to-Mars approach argue that it would be less risky than a sprint and in the long run more rewarding and productive in terms of experience, knowledge gained, and also in terms of the ultimate goal—a permanent manned outpost on Mars.

An artist's conception of the proposed NASA space station Freedom *in Earth orbit. Crew members in shirt-sleeved comfort are at work in one of the two baseline modules, while others engage in extravehicular maintenance.* Freedom *might represent NASA's first real step toward a manned Mars expedition.*

Who?

Once the question of how to go to Mars has been answered, the next inevitable question—Who will go?—will have to be answered as well. In many ways, the second question is more important than the first; the success or failure of the mission will ultimately depend on the performance of the crew. No group of humans have been so far away from home and in such an alien and hostile environment. The distance between the spacecraft and Earth will become so huge that radio communications with ground control will suffer from long delays and even be lost occasionally, leaving the crew to deal with immediate crises without advice and support from Earth. The members of the crew will have only each other to depend on. It is imperative, therefore, that crew members are compatible and that they form a cohesive, working unit that will not fracture or splinter during a journey that might last as long as two and a half to three years. Group dynamics will play a crucial part in a mission to Mars.

What kind of people will be chosen for the voyage to Mars? In the first years of space exploration, NASA and its Soviet counterpart chose their astronauts and cosmonauts exclusively from the ranks of military fighter-jet pilots. These were men with lightning reflexes and steel nerves, accustomed to handling volatile, high-performance aircraft, often in extremely dangerous situations.

The prototype AX-5 space suit is tested underwater at the NASA Ames Research Center in Mountain View, California, in April 1988. The AX-5 is designed specifically as a space station garment. Built entirely of aluminum, the AX-5 will protect a space-walking astronaut from micrometeoroids, harmful solar and cosmic radiation, and the cold vacuum of outer space.

A man who could engage calmly in a supersonic, life-and-death dogfight with a highly trained adversary and then land his damaged fighter jet on the heaving deck of an aircraft carrier—*at night*—was a likely candidate for the astronaut or cosmonaut corps.

But with the advent of long-duration spaceflight and the development of spacecraft that could carry more than one or two passengers, the nature of space exploration and the role of the cosmonaut and astronaut began to change. Pure exploration—simply to go and get back—gave way to scientific exploration, in which observation and experimentation became the focus of an expedition. In 1965, the first two nonpilots journeyed into outer space aboard the Soviet *Voskhod 1* spacecraft. Konstantin Feoktistov was an engineer and spacecraft designer, and Boris Yegorov was a physician. NASA did not begin sending nonpilots into space so soon, but by the mid-eighties U.S. space shuttles were regularly carrying aloft nonpilots, including scientists, schoolteachers, and even politicians.

A Mars vessel might carry a crew numbering anywhere from 4 or 6 to 12, 14, or 15 people, depending on the size of the ship and the duration of the journey. A sprint mission would have fewer crew members than would a later expedition that might be the culmination of an evolutionary Earth-to-moon-to-Mars effort. A smaller crew would have astronauts or cosmonauts who specialized in a certain area of the mission but who were also proficient in many other areas. For example, there might be a woman who functioned as pilot/engineer/physicist and a man who was a copilot/navigator/astronomer. They might be accompanied by a male physician/psychologist/nutritionist and a female computer specialist/communications technician. All four crew members would be trained to pilot the spacecraft if the need arose. The larger the crew, on the other hand, the more room there would be for nonpilot specialists such as physicians, exobiologists, or even someone in charge of filming, videotaping, or otherwise recording the historic journey. All crew members must undergo intensive, long-term training that might last for several years.

There should be a single mission commander—someone, male or female, with absolute authority. This sounds undemocratic and militaristic, but it will be necessary in times of crisis, when decisions need to be made quickly. A competent, authoritative mission commander will also have a stabilizing effect on group dynamics. Interpersonal stresses and strains will be inevitable during a journey in which a number of people are confined in a small area for 15 or 16 months. A mission commander will resolve conflicts, ease friction, and defuse potentially explosive situations between crew members, thus maintaining a stable social order aboard the ship, an especially critical factor for an international, multilingual, or sexually integrated crew.

The physical and mental health of the crew is of the utmost importance. A serious illness or injury in space could have disastrous consequences, and any proposed mission-to-Mars crew must include at least one experienced physician with in-depth training in what has come to be known as space medicine. Psychiatric experience will be invaluable as well. A large crew might include a psychiatrist or psychologist in addition to a physician.

How will the men and women of a Mars mission react emotionally and mentally to their situation? There is much speculation on this matter. The astronauts and cosmonauts of the *Skylab, Salyut,* and *Mir* space stations, some of whom have spent up to a year in outer space, have provided an invaluable source of information on the effects on humans of long-term confinement in a spacecraft. Nuclear submarine crews and people who have spent extended periods at isolated Arctic or Antarctic research stations have been studied as well. So far, the data suggests that members of an interplanetary crew will be subject to a variety of emotional and psychological disturbances, most of them transitory and relatively mild—claustrophobia, earth-separation anxiety, mild insomnia, and mild depression and irritability. Overtired and overworked astronauts or cosmonauts snapping at flight controllers and arguing with each other is a fairly common occurrence, even in flights of only a week or two. But there is also the possibility of more acute and perhaps chronic problems during a long-duration mission—major depression, severe sleep disorders, paranoia, hostility, and even psychosis. In 1985 a *Salyut* cosmonaut named Vladimir Vasyutin became ill on a long-duration mission. Anxiety, insomnia, and loss of appetite led to a a major depressive episode. Vasyutin became incapacitated, and the mission had to be cut short.

The most effective way to prevent such an occurrence is a rigorous psychological screening process for all prospective crew members. This has worked quite well for both NASA and the Soviets so far, but they have also discovered that certain aspects of spaceflight will inevitably give rise to certain problems, no matter how emotionally stable an astronaut or cosmonaut may be. Psychiatrists and psychologists are in the process of developing various possible remedies for these problems. For example, chronic insomnia and other sleep disturbances are known to cause anxiety and depression, and astronauts and cosmonauts frequently suffer from sleep disturbances brought about by disruption of their circadian rhythms. (Circadian rhythms act as a biological clock that tells a person when it is time to go to bed and when it is time to get up, thus establishing a comfortable sleep-wake, work-rest cycle.) Circadian rhythms, in turn, are determined by the daily 24-hour cycle of darkness and sunlight most people on Earth experience. A change in a person's daylight-darkness cycle, such as that experienced by astronauts and cosmonauts in flight, will cause sleep disturbances, which might in turn cause various problematic psychological (as well as physiological) symptoms.

Dr. Charles Czeisler, a Harvard sleep-disorder expert, has been working since 1986 on a method of light therapy that will allow space travelers to keep their biological clock operating on a comfortable schedule. Czeisler's therapy involves exposing a person to timed doses of light of a specific intensity. With this method, a space traveler's biological clock can be reset and regulated so that the subject will have an earthly "night" and "day" phase each 24 hours. The maintenance of a regular earthly sleep-wake cycle, biologically reinforced by light therapy, will

International crews are common in the Soviet space program. In this photo, taken aboard the Salyut 7 space station in 1984, guest cosmonaut Rakesh Sharma of India and Soviet cosmonaut Yury Malyshev demonstrate the effects of weightlessness on Malyshev's countryman Leonid Kizim.

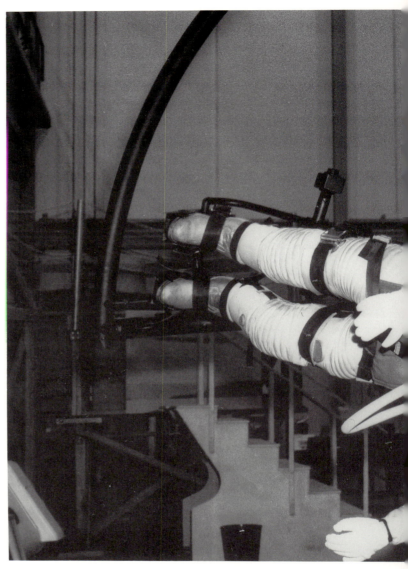

reduce insomnia and other sleep disturbances and thus help to ward off such subsequent, potentially disruptive psychological and physiological symptoms as fatigue, anxiety, and irritability.

Spaceflight is an extremely risky prospect in itself. Interplanetary travelers will face a host of dangers every day,

A NASA engineer demonstrates a zero-gravity simulator at the Manned Spacecraft Center in Houston, Texas. This simulator is one of many devices used by astronauts to get accustomed to working in a zero-gravity environment.

including radiation poisoning and broken bones as well as the ever-present threat of a catastrophic failure of life-support systems or a simple outer-space accident. Other factors that are less immediately threatening but potentially more debilitating in the long run will have to be dealt with as well. A Mars ship will have to carry huge stores of food that will remain both nutritious and appetizing; the ship will also need a reliable waste-disposal system. And the interior of the spacecraft will have to be kept clean. Being confined to a small space for months on end will be difficult enough; being confined to a small, *dirty* space for months on end might become unbearable, not to mention unhealthy.

Extended weightlessness poses a major health risk to cosmonauts and astronauts on long-duration flights. For an astronaut or cosmonaut living for a year or more in a zero-gravity environment, a variety of physiological symptoms will develop and then worsen as time goes on. Without the constant pull of the Earth's gravity to work against, muscles will atrophy. Loss of muscle tone and mass will occur. Even the heart, no longer having to pump against gravity, will shrink and weaken. Space travelers will not be affected by these changes until they return to a gravity field; then they will find themselves to be extremely weak, and even standing up will be difficult for a while. After a weightless period of a year or more it might take someone 2 or 3 weeks to regain full strength, even in the 38 percent gravity of Mars.

The most serious result of extended weightlessness is advanced decalcification in the bones of an astronaut or cosmonaut. The human body responds to a lack of gravity by excreting calcium. Over a period of time the loss of calcium will reduce bone density and skeletal strength. A space traveler will then develop a condition much like osteoporosis—his or her bones will become weak and brittle.

The Soviets have had some success in combating the debilitating effects of life in zero gravity. A high-calcium diet has proved useful. A couple of hours of daily exercise during spaceflight has also helped *Mir* and *Salyut* cosmonauts to ward off the progressive weakening of muscles and bones. The most effective way to prevent zero-gravity syndrome is by providing a spacecraft with artificial gravity. This can be done by rotating the vessel to create centrifugal

force, which will simulate the effects of gravity inside the ship—a difficult and perhaps prohibitively energy-consuming process.

Psychological disturbances, bacterial infections, fires and accidents, broken bones caused by decalcification, loss of muscle mass and strength, micrometeoroids—these are but a small sample of the dangers that Mars-bound travelers will face. But the most menacing, and perhaps the most dangerous, threats to the crew will be those that are as yet unknown and hence impossible to prepare for. In these situations, simple human courage and resourcefulness will be put to the test.

At Moscow's Medical Biology Institute, a Soviet space physician conducts tests on 1 of 10 men who have volunteered to stay in bed for a year. The device on the man's lower torso is called a vacuum suit and is used to underpressurize his legs. The experiment was done to investigate the effects on the human body of long periods of inactivity.

When, Why, and What Next?

When will a manned mission to planet Mars take place? It is apparent that the Soviet Union is committed to a Mars expedition and is currently developing and harnessing the technological and human resources that will make such an endeavor possible. Clearly, its outer space accomplishments in the past two and a half decades are part of a well-conceived, step-by-step plan to put cosmonauts on Mars. Its *Buran* space shuttle (which is virtually identical to NASA's shuttle in design and capabilities), *Energia* booster rockets, *Soyuz* and *Progress* cosmonaut ferries, and *Salyut* and *Mir* expandable space stations represent the most visible evidence of its Mars ambition. Each of these projects is directly applicable to a Mars expedition. Because of their penchant for secrecy, it can safely be assumed that for every outer-space research and development program made public by the Soviets there is another that is still under wraps, so the true extent of their Mars capabilities may be more formidable than they admit. Many observers believe, for example, that the Soviets will soon unveil a nuclear-electric propulsion system that will be used to power a modified *Mir* space station to Mars. A manned Mars flyby by Soviet cosmonauts in a *Mir* spacecraft could occur before the turn of the century, and sources within the Soviet space agency have recently been hinting that the year 2010 may witness the first cosmonauts on Mars.

An artist's conception of a space habitat for 10,000 people. Living and agricultural areas are located in the outer wheel; the hub serves as a command-and-control center and a docking port for incoming spacecraft. More than a mile in diameter, the habitat rotates to provide artificial gravity through centrifugal force. The suspended mirror reflects sunlight onto the various parts of the habitat.

An analysis of their known present-day capabilities does not make a 2010 goal seem farfetched or overly optimistic.

In the United States, momentum is also building toward a manned Mars project. At NASA and other government agencies; at navy and air force testing grounds; in private laboratories, corporate think-tanks, and university seminars, men and women are currently investigating a vast multitude of technological and logistic issues that might be applied to a Mars expedition. Books (such as this one), studies, reports, articles in newspapers and magazines, and television shows, all addressing the mission-to-Mars question, have become abundant in the United States. As in Percival Lowell's time, planet Mars seems to be on everybody's mind. And yet the United States lags well behind the Soviet Union in most areas related to a manned mission to Mars. In particular, the *Energia* booster and the *Mir* space station give the Soviets an undeniable edge. NASA simply does not have anything to compare with these elements of the Soviet manned space program.

Why, then, is America dragging its feet in the terrestrial mud while cosmonauts in Soviet space stations occupy the heavens and prepare themselves for interplanetary adventures? It seems that America is not quite sure about Mars. NASA cannot marshal the necessary resources to send astronauts to Mars unless it receives unequivocal backing—and the subsequent funding—from Congress and the president. NASA estimates that a Mars program following an evolutionary approach will take at least 30 years and cost at least $500 billion. A sprint to Mars might be far less expensive and less time consuming, but a firm commitment to either has yet to appear. Although President Bush has offered executive approval and support and has attempted to establish a loose agenda for an eventual manned expedition to Mars sometime in the next century, Congress remains ambivalent toward the issue.

The first step toward any type of U.S. Mars expedition— the building and deployment of the long-talked-about

Freedom space station, NASA's answer to *Mir*—has been continually delayed, postponed, shelved, canceled, revived, and canceled yet again. Continuing problems with the space shuttle and an embarrassing and costly foul-up with the much ballyhooed Hubble Space Telescope have undermined NASA's most recent attempts to get *Freedom* off the ground. If indeed another space race between the superpowers is developing, the Soviet Union has gotten off to a rather large, and perhaps insurmountable, head start. Nevertheless, the United States has shown in the past an ability to make huge technological leaps. Inspiration and innovation have always been the hallmarks of American outer-space endeavors, and NASA may still be able to mount the kind of brilliant, inspired efforts—such as Project Apollo—that have in the past made the Soviet programs seem plodding, heavy-handed, and inept by comparison.

There has been much speculation about a combined U.S.-USSR Mars expedition. In 1987, Soviet general secretary Mikhail Gorbachev proposed such a partnership but received no positive reaction from the U.S. government. More recently, influential voices in both the United States and the Soviet Union have taken up the call for a joint Mars venture. It is not an unprecedented idea: In July 1975, the two superpowers joined hands in the *Apollo-Soyuz* project. An *Apollo* command module docked with a *Soyuz* spacecraft in Earth orbit and astronauts and cosmonauts visited one another and exchanged gifts. But this was a fairly simple exercise that had more to do with politics than with space exploration.

A combined U.S.-USSR Mars mission would be a far more complicated venture, involving years of cooperation between two longtime adversaries. Although it is an appealing idea, and although each nation has much to offer the other in outer-space expertise and technology, it is not likely to happen. In both nations, space technology is inextricably tangled up with defense technology, and despite *perestroika*, *glasnost*, and the overtures of Gorbachev, neither the Soviet Union nor the United States seems ready for, or willing to participate in, such openness. Astronauts and cosmonauts will go to Mars, but it is doubtful that they will arrive together. This does not preclude some international cooperation and participation in a Mars proj-

ect, however. Japan, China, Eastern European and Soviet satellite nations, Western Europe, Canada, and some South American nations all have growing space programs of their own, and they will all participate in some degree with Soviet or American efforts.

Why should we go to Mars? This question will be asked

Proposed design for NASA's space station Freedom. *The overall configuration is about 500 feet across and 200 feet tall. Eight solar panels will provide about 75,000 watts of electricity. Space shuttles will carry personnel, equipment, and supplies to the station on a regular basis.*

over and over again in the coming years. Indeed, it is this question that is largely responsible for the current indecision in the United States regarding a concerted Mars effort. The idea of spending billions of dollars to put humans on a distant, inhospitable planet does not appeal to everyone. "What is the point?" they ask. "What good will it do us?" The situation on Earth is far from perfect, dissenters point out. Famine, disease, pollution, war, ecological crises, and poverty are but a few of the acute ills that plague our planet as the 21st century approaches. Can we afford to devote so much money, so much thought, and so much effort to such an uncertain quest? Would not our resources be better spent solving our earthly problems and improving the quality of life on our home planet?

Mars advocates have a variety of responses to these questions. The more starry-eyed, romantic members of the pro-Mars faction, our modern-day Lowells, inevitably give the because-it-is-there answer: Humans were born to explore, and a mission to Mars is inevitable, so we should get going. But there is a much better answer, one that is usually given by the more practical Mars advocates. These people point to the benefits that will result from the application of mission-to-Mars related technology to earthly problems.

Everything from medicine to ecological science to the development of new food and energy sources will benefit from a Mars program. For example, research into the spaceflight problem of bone decalcification will be directly applicable to the curing of osteoporosis on Earth. The development of self-sustaining ecosystems to feed humans in a Mars outpost will help in the increasingly vital quest to find new ways to feed Earth's booming population. Mars, the moon, and the other planets and their moons are believed to be mineral rich. Mining operations on these planets and moons could supplement Earth's ever-dwindling supply of minerals.

The space station, space shuttle, and booster technology developed for a Mars mission will have a direct and very positive impact on Earth's energy woes. The Soviet Union is already at work developing gigantic solar panels and mirrors. Deployed and maintained—perhaps by *Energia* boosters and space shuttles—in the correct position above Earth's atmosphere, these gigantic objects will supply light and energy to the vast, dark, and cold Siberian region of the Soviet Union. Extraterrestrial solar light and power technology could significantly reduce the use of fossil fuels—and significantly reduce the subsequent pollution—on Earth. Myriad other potential applications of mission-to-Mars technology are evident, and when they

(continued on page 102)

A return to the moon by humans could result in scenes such as this one, in which astronauts run a lunar mining operation. The purpose of this mine is to produce ilmenite, a mineral common to lunar soil. Ilmenite, when heated, produces water, which in turn, through electrolysis, produces oxygen, which will be breathed by the inhabitants of the moon settlement.

Home Away from Home

Once space travel became a reality, humans began to search for ways to stay in space instead of returning to Earth. In 1971, the Soviet Union placed into Earth orbit its first *Salyut* space station. Since then, orbital habitats have become a staple of the Soviet space program. NASA, however, lags far behind in space station technology and experience. The main reason for this is a lack of public and congressional support and hence a lack of funding for a new space station program. *Skylab*, NASA's first and as yet only space station, was launched in 1973. Inhabited for only 171 days, it eventually fell from orbit, crashing into the Australian outback and the Indian Ocean in 1979 and incurring much negative publicity in the process.

Since the demise of *Skylab*, the American public and Congress have been less than receptive to NASA's proposed Freedom space station program. Many people view space stations as frivolous and unproductive—a motel in outer space where scientists weightlessly putter about, conducting obscure experiments. In truth, however, a permanent space station in Earth orbit as proposed by NASA will play a crucial part in any future manned space exploration undertaken by the United States, such as a return mission to the moon or a mission to Mars. Even more important are the potential applications of *Freedom* to efforts to solve Earth's ever-worsening environmental problems.

A permanently inhabited orbital space station will allow scientists to more effectively monitor global cloud-cover patterns, changes in Earth's vegetation such as the current—and potentially disastrous—defoliation of the Amazon rainforest, the ongoing depletion of the ozone layer, the effects of volcanic eruptions and man-made pollution on weather patterns and other atmospheric conditions, and movements of Earth's tectonic plates, among other things. Clearly, the completion of NASA's Freedom project will help ensure a future not only for the U.S. space program but for planet Earth itself.

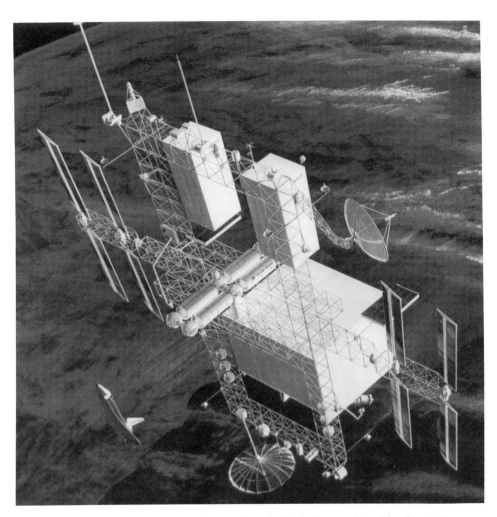

NASA's *proposed space station* Freedom *will probably look something like the station pictured here. A network of trusses supports the various components of this space station, including solar arrays, a power supply module, satellite servicing bays, hangars for various kinds of spacecraft, and habitation and laboratory modules. For a sense of scale, note the arriving space shuttle.*

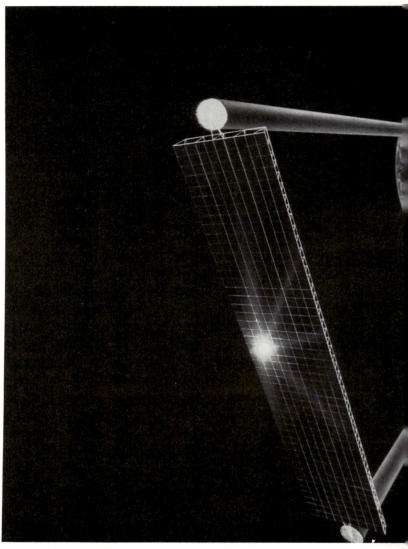

(continued from page 99)
are taken into consideration, a manned expedition to Mars
begins to seem like a necessity rather than a luxury.

What will happen after a spacecraft from Earth sets
down on the surface of Mars? First, the new Martians will
have to learn to survive in that harsh place. Depending
on the nature of their mission, they might stay for a month

With the help of mission-to-Mars related technology, the near future may see the birth of new, extraterrestrial energy sources such as this photovoltaic solar power cell in Earth orbit. The cell is beaming solar energy in microwaves to power stations on Earth. The Energia booster and the space shuttle might be used to deploy and service the power cell.

or they might stay for a year, with a permanent outpost being the ultimate goal. The first visitors will bring their own shelter, oxygen, food, and water supplies. Like nomads clinging to life in a harsh red desert, they will spend weeks or months huddled in crude makeshift shelters made largely from parts of their landing craft. Solar radiation

Like any frontier outpost, the first permanent settlement on Mars will be a stark and uninviting place. But someday, for some humans, it may become home.

and violent wind storms will be their nemeses. Eventually they will be joined or relieved by another mission, and the arduous process of building permanent dwellings and establishing Martian sources of water, food, and breathable air will begin. It is believed that components of the Martian soil will produce oxygen when heated, but establishing permanent food and water resources will be more difficult.

FUEL PLANT

DRILL STATION

CENTRAL POWER SUPPLY

MOBILE STATION

LOGISTICS VEHICLE

MSFC-70-PD-4098

The Martian permafrost might eventually be tapped as a permanent water source, and once a water source is established, self-sufficient habitats with food-producing gardens will begin to spring up like mushrooms. Continually resupplied by manned and unmanned cargo ships plying what *Apollo 11* astronaut Buzz Aldrin describes as the "gravitational trade winds," the outpost will grow, becoming a settlement, then a city. Perhaps it will be called Mars City or Lowell. Like any pioneers, the first Mars settlers will find life in their new environment to be hard and at times unforgiving. There will be accidents, deaths, and tragedies. But one day, if they persevere, a female settler will give birth to a child—the first true Martian.

What next? What comes after Mars? Today a journey to Mars seems like an awesome, near-impossible task. Tomorrow it will be seen as the first step in humankind's expansion into the solar system. The development of colonies on the moon and Mars will ultimately result in new technologies, such as revolutionary propulsion systems that will allow human explorers to travel to the other planets and equipment that will allow them to survive and tame inhospitable new environments. Using the low-gravity Martian moons as staging areas, interplanetary ships will depart for the outer planets. Human space explorers might see the rings of Saturn looming in the windows of their spacecraft; they might build cities on the shores of the nitrogen seas of Triton, one of Neptune's moons; they might set up terraforming operations on one of the 16 moons of Jupiter (terraforming is a process by which a planet or large moon might be given a new, earthlike atmosphere by the introduction of massive alterations, such as an extreme temperature change, to its environment); and finally, perhaps, tiny, frigid Pluto, coated in methane ice and alone at the outer edge of our solar system, will serve as the last outpost for the outward bound—the jumping-off place for points unknown.

Further Reading

Asimov, Isaac. *Mars, the Red Planet*. New York: Morrow, 1977.

Baker, David. *The History of Manned Space Flight*. London: New Cavendish, 1981.

Bond, Peter. *Heroes in Space: From Gagarin to Challenger*. New York: Blackwell, 1987.

Bradbury, Ray. *The Martian Chronicles*. New York: Bantam Books, 1990.

Clark, Philip. *The Soviet Manned Space Program*. New York: Crown, 1988.

Collins, Michael. *Liftoff: The Story of America's Adventure in Space*. New York: Grove Press, 1988.

————. *Mission to Mars*. New York: Grove Wiedenfield, 1990.

Crouch, Tom D. *The National Aeronautics and Space Administration*. New York: Chelsea House, 1990.

Kennedy, Gregory P. *Apollo to the Moon*. New York: Chelsea House, 1992.

————. *The First Men in Space*. New York: Chelsea House, 1991.

McDougall, Walter A. *The Heavens and the Earth: A Political History of the Space Age*. New York: Basic Books, 1985.

Matsunaga, Spark M. *The Mars Project: Journeys Beyond the Cold War*. New York: Hill and Wang, 1986.

Murray, Bruce. *Journey into Space: The First Thirty Years of Space Exploration*. New York: Norton, 1989.

Newkirk, Dennis. *Almanac of Soviet Manned Space Flight*. Houston: Gulf, 1990.

Oberg, James E. *Mission to Mars*. Harrisburg, PA: Stackpole, 1982.

O'Leary, Brian. *Project Space Station*. Harrisburg, PA: Stackpole, 1983.

Osman, Tony. *Space History*. New York: St. Martin's Press, 1983.

Powers, Robert M. *Mars: Our Future on the Red Planet*. Boston: Houghton Mifflin, 1986.

————. *Shuttle: World's First Spaceship*. Harrisburg, PA: Stackpole, 1979.

Smith, Arthur. *Planetary Exploration: Thirty Years of Unmanned Space Probes*. Northamptonshire, England: Patrick Stevens, 1988.

Wells, H. G. *War of the Worlds*. New York: Scholastic, 1972.

Wilford, John Noble. *Mars Beckons*. New York: Knopf, 1990.

Chronology

Entries in roman refer to events directly related to Mars and exploration of the planet; entries in italics refer to important cultural and historic events of the era.

1877	Giovanni Virginio Schiaparelli discovers "canals" on the surface of Mars
1895	Percival Lowell's *Mars* is published; Lowell asserts canals were built by an intelligent race
1911	Konstantin Tsiolkovsky writes *Exploration of Cosmic Space with Reactive Devices*
1926	Robert H. Goddard launches the first liquid-propelled rocket
Oct. 1938	*Orson Welles produces an hour-long radio adaptation of H. G. Wells's* War of the Worlds; *panic ensues in New Jersey as citizens believe the "newscasts" proclaiming Martians were landing in Grovers Mill*
Oct. 1957	Soviets launch first man-made Earth satellite, *Sputnik 1*
1958	The National Aeronautics and Space Administration (NASA) is formed
1960	*John F. Kennedy elected 35th president of the United States*
1961	Yury Gagarin becomes the first human in outer space, in April; Alan Shepard becomes the first American in space one month later; Kennedy declares that the United States should commit itself to landing a man on the moon by the end of the 1960s
Nov. 1963	*John F. Kennedy assassinated; Lyndon Johnson becomes president*
July 1965	*Mariner 4* makes the first flyby of Mars, about 6,000 miles above the Martian surface; the probe transmits pictures and other data back to Earth but finds no evidence of Schiaparelli's canals
1968	*Richard Nixon elected president of the United States*
1969	*Apollo 11* lunar-landing mission; astronauts Neil Armstrong and Buzz Aldrin are the first humans on the moon; *Mariner 6* and *Mariner 7* pass within 2,500 miles of Mars

1971	The Soviet Union launches *Salyut 1*, the first Earth-orbit space station; *Mariner 9* orbits Mars
1972	Apollo program terminated because of public apathy and financial considerations
1973	*Skylab 1* and *Skylab 2* launched into orbit
1974	*Richard Nixon resigns under the shadow of the Watergate scandal*; *Salyut 3* successfully docks with the *Salyut* space station and cosmonauts remain in space for 16 days before returning to Earth; the mission sets the stage for continued Soviet concentration on space-endurance
July–Sept. 1976	*Viking 1* and *Viking 2* land on Mars; the probes send back no evidence of life
1977	First test flight of the space shuttle *Enterprise*; Soviets launch the second generation of the *Salyut* program; make critical advances in solar-energy studies, water-recovery, and extravehicular activity; repeatedly break their own space-endurance records with missions as long as 237 days
1979	*Skylab* falls back to Earth
1980	*Ronald Reagan elected president of the United States*
Apr. 1981	Space shuttle *Columbia* executes first shuttle orbital mission
Jan. 1986	Space shuttle *Challenger* explodes 73 seconds after liftoff; seven astronauts, including a New Hampshire teacher, are killed; Soviets launch the *Mir* space station, the third generation of their space station program
1987	Soviets launch the *Energia* rocket, which can haul almost 10 times the payload of the most powerful American rocket; Soviet leader Mikhail Gorbachev proposes a combined U.S.-USSR mission to put humans on Mars
1988	After a 20-month wait the USS *Discovery* is launched, the first post-*Challenger* launch of the space shuttle; *George Bush elected president of the United States*
2010	Projected year of completion for a sprint mission to Mars
2030	Earliest projected year for an Earth-to-moon-to-Mars mission

Index

Picture Credits

AP/Wide World Photos: p. 87; The Bettmann Archive: pp. 15, 20; JPL/NASA: pp. 65, 66–67, 69 (upper); Lowell Observatory Photograph: p. 19; The National Aeronautics and Space Administration: cover, pp. 12, 24, 26, 29, 30, 32, 35, 36, 41, 42–43, 52–53, 54, 57, 58, 61, 68, 70–71, 72, 76–77, 80–81, 82, 88–89, 92, 96–97, 99, 101, 102–3, 104; Novosti/Sovfoto: pp. 74–75, 69 (lower); From *Le opere di G. V. Schiaparelli*, Science and Technology Research Center, The New York Public Library, Astor, Lenox and Tilden Foundations: pp. 16–17; Sovfoto: p. 25; Tass from Sovfoto: pp. 38–39, 44, 46–47, 50–51, 62, 91; UPI/Bettmann Archive: p. 22

Vincent V. DeSomma is a freelance writer and editor with a B.A. in history and political science from Bethany College, an M.A. in diplomatic history from the University of Vermont, and an M.A. in international affairs from the University of Chicago. He is the author of *Union of Soviet Socialist Republics* in the Chelsea House PLACES AND PEOPLES OF THE WORLD series.

William H. Goetzmann holds the Jack S. Blanton, Sr., Chair in History at the University of Texas at Austin, where he has taught for many years. The author of numerous works on American history and exploration, he won the 1967 Pulitzer and Parkman prizes for his *Exploration and Empire: The Role of the Explorer and Scientist in the Winning of the American West, 1800–1900*. With his son William N. Goetzmann, he coauthored *The West of the Imagination*, which received the Carr P. Collins Award in 1986 from the Texas Institute of Letters. His documentary television series of the same name received a blue ribbon in the history category at the American Film and Video Festival held in New York City in 1987. A recent work, *New Lands, New Men: America and the Second Great Age of Discovery*, was published in 1986 to much critical acclaim.

Michael Collins served as command module pilot on the *Apollo 11* space mission, which landed his colleagues Neil Armstrong and Buzz Aldrin on the moon. A graduate of the United States Military Academy, Collins was named an astronaut in 1963. In 1966 he piloted the *Gemini 10* mission, during which he became the third American to walk in space. The author of several books on space exploration, Collins was director of the Smithsonian Institution's National Air and Space Museum from 1971 to 1978 and is a recipient of the Presidential Medal of Freedom.